Jim (a.k.a. 02330),
To one of the most friendly truck drivers I am greeted by daily - I hope you enjoy the book - Thanks,
Dick Sinnott
(DR. ALDEN)
12-3-14

A GLUTTON FOR PUNISHMENT

I'M ONLY A VOLUNTEER

DR. ALDEN

AuthorHouse™
1663 Liberty Drive
Bloomington, IN 47403
www.authorhouse.com
Phone: 1-800-839-8640

© 2014 Dr. Alden. All rights reserved.

No part of this book may be reproduced, stored in a retrieval system, or transmitted by any means without the written permission of the author.

Published by AuthorHouse   11/04/2014

ISBN: 978-1-4969-5136-6 (sc)
ISBN: 978-1-4969-5137-3 (e)

Any people depicted in stock imagery provided by Thinkstock are models, and such images are being used for illustrative purposes only.
Certain stock imagery © Thinkstock.

This book is printed on acid-free paper.

Because of the dynamic nature of the Internet, any web addresses or links contained in this book may have changed since publication and may no longer be valid. The views expressed in this work are solely those of the author and do not necessarily reflect the views of the publisher, and the publisher hereby disclaims any responsibility for them.

This is dedicated to my 96-year-old mother, Mildred Sinnott, and my father, Henry Alden Sinnott, Jr. who passed away before I completed this book. He loved the game of baseball and he would have enjoyed reading "A GLUTTON FOR PUNISHMENT … I'm Only a Volunteer".

I'd also like to dedicate this book to their great-granddaughters, Camryn (9) and Skylar (5) who didn't get a chance to spend much time with their great-grandfather before his passing.

Contents

Foreword ix
Introduction to the 2014 Edition xiii
Chapter 1 In The Beginning 1
Chapter 2 Play Ball 5
Chapter 3 Stepping Up To The Plate 10
Chapter 4 Grounders And Flies 17
Chapter 5 Defining A Coach 20
Chapter 6 Fundraising 24
Chapter 7 Evaluations 27
Chapter 8 The Major League – My First Year 34
Chapter 9 Putting Together A Program 38
Chapter 10 Practice Makes Perfect 47
Chapter 11 Who's On First? 53
Chapter 12 Put Me In Coach 60
Chapter 13 Line Drives 70
Chapter 14 Playoffs 74
Chapter 15 All-Stars - A Summer Of Fun (Usually) 79
Chapter 16 All-Stars - The Long, Action-Packed Summer ... 90
Chapter 17 Child Abuse? 117
Chapter 18 The Graduate 129
Chapter 19 Building The Fields Of Dreams 132
Chapter 20 Maintaining The Fields - The Good Guy 138
Chapter 21 Maintaining The Fields- The Visitors 154
Chapter 22 Maintaining The Fields- The Bad Guy 160
Chapter 23 ADHD 171
Chapter 24 Extra Innings 173

Foreword

Many times over the years I have been asked if Dick Sinnott is my brother. When I replied that he is, I would be told that he had coached the speaker's child in youth baseball. I knew that he had coached for many years, but I had not realized the depth of his involvement until I read this book. He has been a positive influence in the lives of many local children.

I also knew that for many years he had mowed the ball fields, but I didn't realize how much additional work was involved in keeping them in good shape.

My brother doesn't talk a lot about what he does; he just goes ahead and does it.

Almost three years ago, he approached me about proofreading his book. That was the first I knew about any book! I agreed to share the job with my nephew Jared. In the process, I learned a great deal about youth baseball – and my brother. If you have ever wondered about what goes on before the players go out on the field, read this book. You will learn much about hard work and dedication.

Linda Merritt

Hundreds of kids have called my father Coach. I am amazed by all of the people who still refer to my father as Coach. Grown men not much younger than my father, my own peers, and kids much younger than I; it always seems there is someone calling my dad Coach. I've been out to eat with my parents and random people have come to say hi to "Coach," and ask how he is doing. He follows their baseball careers proudly, and even has updates for when they make it to high school and college baseball. Many of my friends still refer to him as Coach - not Dick, not Mr. Sinnott, but Coach. Through twenty-five years of coaching baseball, and even a stint leading a local youth basketball league dynasty, my father has impacted many lives, and, in my opinion, been a strong face in the community.

His coaching style is laid back; he is definitely more Terry Francona than Earl Weaver. He trusts his players and wants them to have fun. Rarely raising his voice, he often lightens the mood in a high pressure situation with a joke or a confidence booster. I am always amazed by, and sometimes confused by, his total dedication to his teams and his players. Whether holding batting practice in a gymnasium in January or getting his kids to the field at 7:30 AM on a Saturday for pregame batting practice in July, he always gives his teams everything he can. His vacation time is often used to get to tournaments early or for when there is a rain date. He loves Middleboro and has helped generations of kids enjoy youth sports and know the joy and confidence that comes from being part of a team.

I didn't play baseball for him much after tee ball, I believe only one year, but I am still proud of what he has done. I remember vividly when he coached a rival team and playing against him was the biggest game of my season. I hate to say, but I am pretty sure my team won that matchup.

He was my coach in basketball for many years, and those were very fun. He let my friends and me run wild at times, but he always reeled us in when a big stop was needed or a key offensive play had to be diagrammed.

Dr. Alden

The dynasty I mentioned was actually one I was a part of. My team won 3 straight championships—a 3peat, if you will—during my high school years. The first year we started out very slowly. We didn't play particularly well and became known for our on-court antics. We had players shoot free throws underhand, bench players run onto the court during game action to celebrate, a player kick the ball as though it were a field goal attempt… you get the idea. Mind you we did this blatantly and to entertain each other, not out of ignorance. One upping each other and pushing the comedic boundaries almost became a separate game to us. It was bedlam. But Coach had us buckle down, instituted a few plays, and appealed to our pride.

Sure enough, we went on a nice run and won the championship. We were made up completely of players at the younger end of the age spectrum, a team of 15-year-olds beating teams with many 16- and 17-year-olds on it. We really had no business, talent wise, winning that first title, but Coach led us to glory and gave us memories we still talk about today when we get together. We had a great time together but played as a team when we really needed to. We even had a small following of friends and family that would come watch our games, not typical in the league we were in. I really believe people enjoyed watching us because my father allowed us to have fun as if we were playing pick-up ball but regimented enough to keep us playing winning basketball. To me, that is the balance youth sports should strive for and coaches should nurture.

There is one other story about that basketball team that I really enjoy and says a lot about my father as a coach and leader. In the excitement of possibly winning a third championship in a row, I had started to get sloppy and be a showboat. At one point I attempted a couple of behind the back passes (I watched too much Sportscenter). He immediately took me out of the game. He was willing to bench me in our last championship defense because I was putting myself ahead of the team. He wanted us to have fun but also wanted to teach us that unselfishness is the key to being a part of any team. He didn't play favorites, not even with his son. I respect that. You earn your spot and he empowers you to be your best.

So I am jealous of all the kids that still get to call him Coach. I guess I'll have to settle for sharing him with all the other kids that he has mentored. I hope they all know how lucky they are to call him Coach.

Jared Sinnott

Introduction to the 2014 Edition

This book may be of interest to anyone planning to become involved with a Youth Baseball Program. When I first became involved with the program, children began playing baseball at the age of six, but within the past few years, children could begin playing at the age of five. The book will give parents an idea of what they and their children may experience during their years with Youth Baseball, from tee ball on through the major league. I'm sure it will also provide a few good laughs.

My experiences are probably quite similar to those who have coached Youth Baseball in almost any town. An individual hoping to manage or coach a team or one that is recruited to help coach a team may also learn a lot about what can happen during the course of a season. Those individuals having previously managed or coached a team of another sport may already be aware of what to expect. Additionally, an individual pondering the thought of becoming involved with maintaining ball fields will find out what they may encounter if taking on the field maintenance position. Hopefully, after reading about what I dealt with myself while maintaining the fields, I will not scare away any future prospects.

Dick Sinnott

Middleborough, Ma.
October 2014

1

IN THE BEGINNING

My name is Dick, and my wife's name is Sue. I was at home painting the walls of what would soon be our second child's bedroom. My wife and I had selected a color which would be acceptable for either a boy or a girl. Those were the days before an expectant mother could choose whether or not to have an ultrasound prior to birth to determine the baby's gender. The color we chose for the room was a green similar to the color of the Boston Red Sox Fenway Park's left field wall which was commonly known as "The Green Monster". We were already the parents of a lovely daughter, Tara, who was five years old. We were thankful that she was a beautiful and healthy child. I was like most guys who had hoped for a son but upon her arrival I was ecstatic. I believed that I still had a chance at a later date to father a son.

As I applied the final coat of paint to the last wall in the room, my wife came in and informed me that she had to get to the hospital immediately. I told her I was just about finished, and I couldn't stop at that moment. I said I would be done in just a few minutes and then we could go. She was a bit upset with me and told me to hurry up unless I wanted to deliver the baby. I promptly finished the wall and cleaned up. I figured it wouldn't be smart to waste as much time as I had before heading to the hospital the day my daughter was born.

That day, I was also working on a project at home when my wife informed me that we had better head over to the hospital right away. I finished what I was doing, but proceeded to put together a couple of tuna fish sandwiches to take with me to the hospital. I had been working hard all day, and I needed some nourishment.

We eventually headed to the hospital and when we arrived, my wife proceeded to check in for her admission to the maternity ward. Once she was settled, I decided to eat my sandwiches. I probably should have chosen peanut butter and jelly sandwiches because all you could smell in my wife's room and the hallway was tuna fish. It really wasn't what you would call a pleasant aroma. My wife went through the normal process of labor pains, contractions, and delivery without many problems. From the time we left the house until the actual delivery, a total of three-and-one-half hours had elapsed. So what was the big rush?

The day our second child was born, a total of four hours had elapsed from the time we left the house until the baby's grand entrance. Again, there was more than enough time.

Our second child arrived sporting an appendage that our first child did not have. Yes, it was a boy! To this day, I feel that not knowing the baby's gender until its arrival into this world was more of a thrill than knowing within the first few months of conception. I will never forget either of my children's grand entrances.

The first thought in my mind was that I now had a son who we named Jared, and that someday he would be playing sports, whether it was baseball, basketball or football. It would only be a matter of time before I could start the teaching process. I never figured my son would be a professional athlete but only hoped that he could enjoy playing sports as I did. I had heard that only 1 in 16,000 children ended up playing professional sports, so I never got my hopes up.

There was plenty of time to work with my son since he would have to be six years old before he could play organized sports. I had introduced sports to my daughter when she was young, and she chose to play soccer for only one year. I didn't push sports on her, but let her decide for herself what she wanted to do. She took classes in dance and cheerleading and joined the Brownies. Her favorite pastime was singing. She participated in the church's junior choir and later became involved with various high school choruses and the high school's yearly entertainment show. She kept very busy as a child and enjoyed what she did. She always told me that sports were for boys. As long as she did have fun, that's all that mattered.

It was only a matter of a year or so before I bought my son his first baseball glove, baseball bat, and baseball. Years later, with my two granddaughters, I couldn't wait that long. I had snuck a baseball and baseball glove to my daughter's baby shower for my first granddaughter, Camryn. My second granddaughter, Skylar received her baseball and baseball glove the day she came home from the hospital after her birth. With my son, I figured that when he was able to walk, it was time to start teaching him the game. My son and I spent a lot of time in the back yard working on the basics of the game. We played catch over and over until I became the one who got tired and wanted to take a break. I did not push him as much as he pushed me.

Once he got pretty good at catching the ball, I thought we could try a little fielding. The most important rule in fielding was to move his feet and to get himself in front of the ball. Trying to explain that to a young child was difficult. I didn't expect him to learn overnight so I just had to be patient. The next most important rule in fielding was to bend the knees and keep the glove close to the ground so the ball wouldn't sneak underneath and get by. It was amazing how little space was needed between the glove and the ground for a baseball to elude you. I kept reminding him of the well-known phrase "practice makes perfect". The next phase of the game we worked on was batting. The first bat he used was more like a fat club, like that a cave man would carry. It really didn't look like a baseball bat. The good thing about it was that the ball that came with it was the size of a softball which made it much easier for a young child to hit. Being made of plastic was a good idea since a youngster could hit the ball much easier than if he used a regulation-sized baseball bat and baseball. It would discourage a child if he couldn't make contact with the ball, causing him to lose interest in the game quickly.

We continued to play baseball, not only at home, but at the baseball park where he would eventually play. My son kept asking me how much longer before he could play real baseball and was upset when I told him not until he was six years old.

I didn't tell him that he would start off playing tee ball his first year before eventually playing "real" baseball a few years later. I only imagined how upset he would have been had I told him he would have to wait until he was eight years old. When he entered the first grade, he expected that he would finally be able to play organized baseball. His friends were talking about the arrival of spring and the beginning of baseball practice. Unfortunately, when sign-ups arrived, we found out that he would not be old enough to play with most of his friends. They would have turned six

Dr. Alden

years old before the July 31st cut-off date, and he wouldn't turn six years old until October. He would have to wait another year before he could play baseball, and he was devastated. It would be a long year's wait until the next spring, and in the meantime there was one upset son and one upset dad.

2

PLAY BALL

Finally the day arrived when a notice was sent home from school informing us as to when and where we could sign up our son to play baseball. This was the day he had been waiting for, the day when a young boy could play America's National Pastime. He waited patiently for the day to officially sign up to play organized baseball. We arrived along with many other smiling six-year- olds who were waiting in line for this special day. It was only February and it would be another six to eight weeks before practices would begin. This would give us plenty of time to purchase any equipment needed for our son's first practice. He already had a bat and glove, but still needed a pair of baseball pants, socks, and cleats. The game shirt and a hat would be provided by the league.

As the weather started to get better, we had a chance to get outside a few times to loosen up before his first scheduled practice. The season of spring no longer seemed to exist here in New England since winter would usually go right into summer. Explaining that to a six-year old was difficult since a child looked forward to spring knowing that it meant baseball would be starting soon.

It finally arrived – the first day of practice. I packed up the family and headed to the ball field which was located at the town's local playground. The manager of the team introduced himself to each family as they arrived. He had each player sit on the bench for a team meeting once everyone arrived. First he told everyone the name of the team they would be playing on – it was sponsored by a local rubbish removal company. The players and their parents didn't show any sign of enthusiasm when it was announced. The manager agreed that he would have been happy with most any sponsor with the exception of the one whose company pumped out cesspools and septic tanks. The nickname for that team in years past was "The Kakka Suckers". Everyone agreed with the point he made and graciously accepted our assigned sponsor's name. He explained to the players and parents what he hoped to accomplish during the season. Teaching the fundamentals of the game would be most important. He stressed that when they played a game against another team, the goal was to learn the game of baseball and to have fun. The score was not as important as becoming a better ball player. There would be no "standings" to compare records and there would be no playoffs or champions at the tee ball level. That comment pretty much put the kids in shock, since they couldn't understand why the score wasn't kept so they could tell everyone who had won the game. After all, don't you play any type of game in the hopes of being the winner? The manager made it very clear to the parents that they would follow the rules as well.

Next on the manager's agenda was the solicitation for parents to volunteer with assisting him. There was no response. The parents, including myself, must have thought it wouldn't be difficult for one individual to teach the game of baseball to 15 six- and seven-year- olds for an hour and one half. He pleaded for at least one volunteer before asking if I would assist him. He said someone had given him my name as a possible candidate to help coach.

I said I was really not interested, since I didn't know much about coaching baseball. I had played baseball as a child, and I was currently playing in a men's softball league. I couldn't get him to understand that I would rather observe than coach. After a few minutes, I gave in and said I would give it a try. My job would be to place the tee ball on the tee, then give the kids the O.K. to swing the bat and hit the ball. The first boy to bat barely waited for me to place the ball on the tee before he started to swing. I had to jump back out of the way or I would have been writhing in pain in my mid-section. From that point on, I told each boy to wait for me to place the ball on the tee, let me step back, keep his eye on the ball, and wait for me to tell him when to swing. I seriously thought about purchasing a protective cup to shield my "family jewels". Instead, I just paid a little closer attention to each swing of the bat.

Wooden bats had pretty much been phased out from youth baseball at this time, yet there was still one in the team bag along with three or four aluminum bats. The kids used either one of the team bats or brought along one of their own. There was one boy who brought his own wooden bat which looked as if it had been sitting out in a barn for twenty-five years. It had dried out and was very rough and looked as though if you slid your hands along the handle, you would get a handful of splinters. It was thirty-two inches long and much too heavy for a seven-year- old. I suggested that he try using a newer aluminum bat five or six inches shorter and also much lighter, but he wanted no part of it.

I didn't disagree, and I told him to go ahead and use his own bat. His first swing sent the ball out to the center field fence which was a good one-hundred and fifty feet away. He continued to use his own bat and hit the ball solidly every time. He didn't seem to have any problem getting the bat around to hit the ball off the tee, but if I pitched to him I doubted that he would have been able to hit the ball. If I had let him try hitting a live pitch, he probably would have hit a line-drive right back at my head, knowing my luck.

Finally, after numerous practices, it was time for Opening Day. There was a parade every year starting from an adjacent school parking lot which proceeded down the street to the baseball complex. The Opening Day Ceremony began with the President of a local bank, who was very involved with the league, who introduced every player starting with the Tee Ball division all the way through to the Major League division. It was attended by hundreds of parents, siblings, relatives, and friends. As each team was announced, the players, manager and coaches ran out onto the field and assembled for the festivities. Once the National Anthem had been sung and the "First Pitch" had been thrown and the foul line on the grass was re-painted due to the hundreds of ball players having worn it off while running onto the field as their teams were introduced, it was finally time for the season to officially begin. To this day, the same individual is invited back every year to introduce the hundreds of children who will be playing baseball for the upcoming season. He always graciously accepts the invitation and does a fantastic job.

Once the season began, there would be practices during the week along with one week-day game and one game on Saturdays, for a total of 21 games for the season. I went with the flow and did what I was asked to do by the manager that year. My son and I survived the year, and we both had a lot of fun. The parents had followed the rules as the manager had asked. There was a manager from another team who decided not to follow the rules. He kept score of the games as well as the standings. He told his team they were the best team, and they had gone undefeated for the season. Some guys just didn't get it.

My son had completed his first year of tee ball, and February of the next year had arrived. Again, a flyer had been sent home from school for any child interested in playing baseball so he or she could register to play in the upcoming season. My son would be playing in the Tee Ball division again, since it was a two-year program. He was a step closer to playing real baseball, yet still enjoyed the tee ball program. We waited patiently for the day to sign up again, and we were the first ones in line to register. Once he was registered, and as we were about to leave, an individual with the league who was assisting with sign-ups asked if I would be interested in assisting the manager again for the upcoming season. The manager from the previous year's team would be coaching the team again and had hoped I could help him again. We would have the same six-year- olds from the previous year's team, provided they signed up again. We would also be able to choose the players we needed to fill the roster for the team.

I agreed to help coach again, and my son and I couldn't wait until the first practice which was still six or eight weeks away. Once the weather was good, I got outdoors with my son a few times to prepare for the first practice. I hoped the weather would stay nice so my son could get in a few weeks of fielding and batting. The manager and I attended the meeting where we selected the additional players to fill the roster. Then he called all of the players to inform them when the first practice would be held. On the first day of practice, the manager held the team meeting as he did the previous year. The name of the company that was sponsoring the team this year was not much better than the previous year. It happened to be a local funeral home. Again, everyone was not overly happy, but the manager reminded them that it could have been much worse had we been assigned to the team known as "The Kakka Suckers". Again, everyone agreed. This year the manager was very lucky when he asked if there were any additional parents interested in helping to coach the team. Immediately, a parent stepped forward, showing intense enthusiasm or Pie (the Parent with Intense Enthusiasm) as I will refer to him, hereafter. Pie was very excited about coaching and offered many helpful ideas. He had a son on the team and two younger children who would eventually be playing baseball. He was a very nice individual and a "good catch".

The team went on to have another fun year while learning a lot about baseball. I also learned a lot more about coaching. The toughest thing about coaching at the tee ball level was keeping the player's attention. The kids loved to dig holes in the field with their cleats and would dance around in the field while waiting for the ball to be hit. They were loaded with energy, so when they hit the ball, they would keep running the bases all the way to home plate instead of stopping at a base once the ball was thrown into the infield. It turned into a game of "catch me if you can." It was definitely not the type of baseball I was accustomed to. Most important though, the kids had fun. The parents seemed to enjoy watching them, and the kids learned a lot. Although on the other hand, a mother once told me, "Watching a tee ball game was like watching paint dry".

3

STEPPING UP TO THE PLATE

The following year my son advanced to the Farm League division where he finally could play real games. He hit balls that were pitched to him and was allowed to keep score. I had the opportunity to watch his games from the sidelines as a spectator, since he went to a team that already had a manager and enough coaches so that I was not needed to help. My son was also happy that the sponsor of his team was a local auto body shop and not one of the three most dreaded teams to be on, two of which he had previously played on.

The manager who had coached my son's tee ball team had moved along with his son to Farm League. His son had gotten on a different team than my son and he was asked to help the manager of that team. I was asked by Pie, who had coached with me on the previous year's tee ball team, if I would manage the team along with him for another year, since his son had one more year of tee ball left to play. Since I was not managing my son's team, I agreed only if the league could work out a schedule where the two team's games would not conflict. The schedules were made to accommodate my request, so now I could coach tee ball another year.

At the first practice, we held our team meeting stating our intentions of what we hoped to accomplish. We had many ideas to use for practices, and we were ready to go. Each year had become easier to coach, and it was another successful year of tee ball in which both players and coaches enjoyed the game. My son had a great time playing real baseball, and he was already looking forward to the next year.

The following year, Pie's daughter and my niece both wanted to play tee ball, so I agreed to coach tee ball another year. This would be my fourth year coaching tee ball, and my third year with Pie. Pie's son moved up to the Farm League division, and Pie became the manager of his son's team. My son moved up to the Minor League division and as happened the previous year, the manager and coaches were already in place. Once again, the league accommodated both Pie and me by setting up the game schedules so there were no conflicts. We were both very busy since each of us was involved with two teams, but we didn't mind since we both loved baseball.

Prior to the start of the season, the Vice President of the league asked if the two of us would be interested in taking over a Minor League team. He had been informed by some parents of the team that during a practice, the first-year manager had nonchalantly walked out to center field, urinated, then returned to coaching as though nothing had happened. Needless to say, the short-lived tenure of the manager came to an end. There was no assistant coach who might have taken over the team if asked, so we both agreed to take the team. The only problem was that I would be managing a team in the same division that my son was playing in. I agreed that when our team played my son's team, I would just watch the game from the sidelines and let my coaching partner run the team. There were only two games when they played each other during the season, yet I was very uncomfortable just watching those games, since I had a common interest in both teams. That season we spent every day on the fields either practicing or playing games. With me managing two teams and following a third team, and my coaching partner managing three teams, we only had a few conflicts. With the help of our assistant coaches we managed to pull through. It was a long and tiring year but when you loved the game of baseball like we did, it didn't matter. We were there for the kids.

My fifth year was less hectic. My niece was not interested in playing a second year of tee ball, and there were no more friend's or relative's children who would be playing at the tee ball level - thank God. I enjoyed coaching tee ball, yet I thought two years would have been sufficient. After four years of coaching tee ball, I considered myself lucky to still have my fingers intact as well as my other body parts. I volunteered to take the manager's position of my son's Minor League team allowing me to coach a team that I picked on my own, therefore starting out with a clean slate unlike the previous year's inherited team.

I knew one of the father's of one of the children I picked for my team, and he agreed to be my assistant coach. As in the previous year, bunting and stealing were allowed, scores and standings were kept, and at the end of the regular season there were playoffs. I was psyched and so were the players.

The first day of practice was like a tryout. The players first paired up and played catch. This told me a lot about each player. It showed me who could throw the ball and who could catch the ball. Not every child could do both. Next came some fielding drills. I hit baseballs to each child at the shortstop's position. The child then fielded the ball and made a throw to the first baseman. Next I hit fly balls to see how well they could track down the ball. Then I had them throw the ball back to me to see how strong their arms were. I ended practice with some running of the bases. How fast a child ran helped me determine what position a child might be best at on the field and how well he might do as a base runner. A lot of knowledge had been obtained after just one practice, and things were looking good. Every practice thereafter, we would add different drills.

It was suggested by the league that the coaches give each player the opportunity to play both infield and outfield positions and not place the same individuals in the same positions every game. At this level of play, some players could get seriously hurt if playing an infield position. A player must be able to protect himself when playing in the infield where the ball moves quickly both when thrown or hit. The reason a coach plays certain individuals in the outfield is for their own safety and not because they are favoring certain players that play infield positions. Most parents understand the reasoning, yet some do not.

I feel that the most dangerous position to play in the infield is the pitcher. A ball can be hit back to the pitcher very quickly, and the pitcher must have good reflexes since he is the closest fielder to the batter. I give every child the opportunity to prove whether or not he may be a candidate to pitch. Every child wants to be a pitcher, yet every child was not made to be. There was a pitcher on an opposing team who was a tall, lanky left-hander with very poor ball control. He threw the ball very hard but you never knew which way the ball would go. Batters were not afraid of the speed at which he threw the ball but were afraid of not knowing its direction. No one ever wants to get hit by a baseball since the pain, swelling, and bruising that one incurs is not the most pleasant experience. Within two years the "Southpaw" improved his control and made it to the Major League division. As he got older, he improved his accuracy and turned out to be a very good pitcher. He was one of the best pitchers in high school, went on to play at a well-known Division One College, and then was drafted by a professional Major League baseball team.

The next year my son was chosen to play in the Major League division. The manager of the team already had the coaches he needed, so I took the opportunity to observe and learn more about coaching from my son's new coach. My son was very excited at having made the team, and I was also glad that he would have someone coaching him other than me. He always thought he could get away with more when I was coaching, and I felt it would do him good. It was great coaching my son, but sometimes a child benefits more from an outsider.

I was elected to the position of Player Agent for the League which granted me a seat on the Board of Directors that year. The Player Agent from the previous year made a trip out to my house to drop off everything he had which was related to the job. The trunk of his car was loaded to the max. There was a keyboard, a monitor, and an outdated computer which had been installed with an outdated program. He did not have a printer to go with the set up, but at least I could get started. He also pulled out boxes upon boxes of birth certificates which had been with the league for probably six or seven years, of which 90% were useless to me. I had quite a project of sorting them out but I filed the current ones according to age and had a nice bonfire with the remaining boxes.

The computer with its program, Windows 3.1 was only capable of storing information. I was not too familiar with computers so I bought a guide, Windows 3.1 for Dummies, to help me understand how it worked. I did the best I could with what I had and entered the information for each player in the league into the computer. Before I found a printer to hook up to the computer to print out the information, the computer crashed, and I lost everything I had entered. I gave up on the computer and went back to the good old pencil and paper along with my old fashioned typewriter. It worked perfectly and I was happy.

I still wanted to continue coaching, so I agreed to take on a team in the Minor League division again. The league again worked out a game schedule in such a way that my son's games and my team's games did not conflict. I kept plenty busy attending the practices and games for both teams and enjoyed not having to work tee ball into my schedule. My son loved playing at the Major League level, and he felt that he had finally reached his goal. I was happy for him and hoped he would have as much fun the following year. I was happy coaching a Minor League team, and I had a good season.

When the season ended, one of the Major League's managers resigned, which created the opening of his position. It would be my son's final season in the league, and I debated whether or not I should apply for the position. If I was chosen as the manager, I would have the opportunity to move my son onto the team from his previous team. I wasn't sure what to do, but my wife urged me to apply since she knew I really enjoyed coaching. I decided to apply for the position, and I prepared myself for an interview in front of the Board of Directors. The team that had been vacated was sponsored by a local club which I belonged to and was also the same team my father-in-law had coached thirty-five years earlier. I thought it would be nice to be chosen to manage that team for those two reasons. The day of the interview I was a little nervous and hoped I would be the lucky candidate. The interview went well, yet I was not chosen. The candidate that was chosen was none other than my friend Pie, who like me was also on the Board of Directors. I was very happy for him, and he was very excited.

The following season my son played his final year in the Major League division on the same team he had played on the previous year. Once a player is selected for a team in the Major League, he or she continues to play on that team through his or her twelve- year-old year. This would be his last year before he would move up to the next level of baseball.

I was re-elected to the position of Player Agent and decided to stay involved with coaching. I threw away my pencil and paper, packed away my old fashioned typewriter, and took a trip to the dump with the outdated computer system. The league purchased a completely new and modern computer system, on which a woman involved in the league and familiar with computers agreed to input all of the information for the league's players. It probably took her one-tenth of the time that it took me the previous year. The capabilities of the new system made both her life and my life much easier.

I chose to stay with the Minor League Division again since it was a lot of fun. Occasionally a player was chosen to move up to the Major League division from the Minor League division to fill an opening. Whenever that happened, it gave the manager of the Minor League team the feeling that he had helped develop the player. It was upsetting in a sense to lose a very good player, yet you were happy to see the player advance.

A Glutton For Punishment

My first day of practice was the day I referred to previously as a try-out. I had just begun the drill in which the player at shortstop fielded the ball and would then throw the ball to the first baseman. Wouldn't you know the first ball thrown to the first baseman bounced off his glove, hit him in the mouth, and knocked out one of his teeth. Luckily, it was a baby tooth. It did not seem to bother him, and he continued to practice. The reason the child had a problem catching the ball was because he was wearing a small vinyl baseball glove which he could barely fit his hand into. It was a glove suitable for a two-year old and not a ten-year old. I recommended that his parents purchase a full-sized leather baseball glove before the next practice.

The team played some pretty good baseball and improved as the season progressed. My toothless player struggled, not only with catching but also with batting. He could not hit the ball to save his soul. He was so discouraged with himself during one game, he decided that before the baseball came across home plate while he was batting, he would lean forward with his head over the plate, so the baseball would hit him in the head, resulting in being awarded first base since he had been hit by the pitch. He was so happy he finally got a chance to get on base, he jumped up and down all excited and headed to first base. I went over to see if he was ok and told him never do that again, since he could get seriously injured. I explained to his parents what he had told me, and luckily for me they were very understanding.

After the game ended, the Vice President of the league, who happened to be watching the game, came over to me and asked me why I let my players get on base that way. I told him I would never tell a batter to do that, and I explained to him the reason my player did it. The following year the league required that all helmets have a metal cage to protect the player's face should they be hit by the ball. It was a good idea for safety's sake.

Another season came to an end, and my son completed his seventh year of Youth Baseball. I wondered what it would be like not coaching any longer and what would come next. Within a few weeks upon completion of the Major League division playoffs, another Major League division manager resigned. My son would not be playing any longer in the league yet I contemplated whether or not I should apply for the position. My wife told me I should try again since I really enjoyed coaching. She felt I had a good chance of getting the position since I put a lot of time in coaching and since I had just completed my second term as the Player Agent. The team with the opening was sponsored by a local insurance company which was owned by the brother of one of my best friends I'd known since I was a young child. I attended the interview and was chosen to manage the team. This was the day my life officially started to be taken over by the Youth Baseball league. I was very excited and couldn't wait to begin. The managers of the Major League division in our town often continue coaching even after their child has moved on to the next level of play. We are a baseball town, and many coaches stay with the program for the love of the game. Over half of the managers coaching in the Major League division do not have children of their own on their team. In fact, there were numerous managers and coaches in the league never having any children of their own on the team they coached.

The following season, now being a Major League manager, I could not hold the position of Player Agent. Instead, I accepted the nomination and was elected to the position of Purchasing Agent. I first made a trip to the storage facility which the league rented to store all of the equipment during the off-season. There were shelves of old equipment and equipment bags which I had to go through and pull out the defective equipment. The league purchased a lot of new equipment that year, mostly for safety reasons. Over the course of the season, I was responsible for purchasing whatever equipment was necessary. To make it easier for me or my successor the next year, I put together a notebook that gave a step-by-step guide of what and when to purchase during the season. It would make the position of Purchasing Agent as simple as could be. The following year, the individual that took over the position didn't seem very interested with the work I had done to make the job easier and he threw away the notebook. He never had the equipment that was needed until it was too late, and many items he never ordered. He would have looked like a genius had he kept the notebook which I had prepared. I would have appreciated a step-by-step guide the year I had taken over the position, but instead I had to learn the hard way. My successor never learned.

4

GROUNDERS AND FLIES

I had learned a lot about coaching and also realized that the lower the level of play, the less the children stayed focused. The Major League level was for the serious baseball players; and if they didn't want to take it seriously they should play at a lower level.

Tee ball players, being only six and seven years old, had the shortest attention span. Anything could distract a player on the bench or on the field. There was a lot of down time in between swings of their bats, giving them plenty of time for their minds to wander. Picking a bouquet of dandelions for Mom or performing a series of cartwheels, somersaults and banana twirls were the most common activities in between swings. Other distractions included playing around ant hills or playing with night crawlers, toads, and frogs. Animals such as squirrels and rabbits or cats and dogs also visited the ball fields causing a commotion and slowing down the game. Once, a family of ducks marched proudly across the outfield during a game – needless-to-say, there were always bees, dragonflies and butterflies making a visit.

The most annoying distraction occurred when a flock of geese flew overhead in perfect formation and decided to practice dropping bombs. As luck would have it, a bomb plopped on my head, which luckily was covered by my hat. It was a direct hit, and I honestly believe the honking noise they made as they flew overhead was actually them laughing at me. That incident was a perfect example as to why all ballplayers should ALWAYS wear a hat while playing baseball.

The biggest distraction of all came one day during a Minor League game. We were in the middle of a game at a field in the outskirts of town when we had to put a temporary hold on the game. It was about 10:00 A.M. in the morning on a day when there was an afternoon air show scheduled to be held at an Air Force Base which was approximately thirty miles away. The baseball field we were playing on happened to be directly below the flight path of the aircraft en route to the base where they would be on display. The umpire had to stop the game while the players, coaches, and spectators had their own private air show. Everyone tried to get a good view of the aircraft by moving to be directly under the aircraft. If only ball players would position themselves under a fly ball during a game to make a catch the way they moved to get a close look at the aircraft, maybe more balls would be caught. The most fascinating aircraft to everyone was the Stealth Bomber. It flew above the ball field so quietly you barely knew it was there. The aircraft definitely had an appropriate name. On the other hand, when the enormous DC-3 transport plane flew overhead, you could feel the vibration as it passed by. There was also a B-52 bomber, an F-15 fighter jet, and a harrier craft. Also making an appearance were a few vintage bi-planes, which were quite colorful. There were also other aircraft which I could not identify. I knew the names of so many of the aircraft because I had been to an air show the previous summer and seen many of the same aircraft I saw pass over the ball field.

There were many other occasions where players, coaches and spectators were distracted. There once was a serious automobile accident involving a teenage driver and his teenage passengers, which occurred not far from the ball field. The usual police cruisers, ambulances and fire trucks which responded drew some attention; but it was a med-flight helicopter, which was called in to transport the injured parties, that caused concern. It was amazing how everyone lost focus in the game. The accident actually caused a slight delay.

A very common distraction was when a student airplane pilot was being given lessons on equipment failure drills, such as what they call engines-out. What happens is that everyone sees and hears an airplane flying overhead, when all of a sudden the motor shuts down. Everyone panics thinking the plane is going to crash as it starts gliding into a descent, yet within a few seconds the motor starts up again and the plane flies away. There is an airport located in the next town, and for some reason the most popular spot for this training is directly over the ball fields. I have seen this happen many times during both practices and games and wonder why we are so lucky to have the training held directly above our heads.

There was another incident involving a military helicopter during the winter months which did not affect any players, coaches or spectators. As the helicopter was returning to the military base, it developed engine trouble. It turned out to be a leak in the fuel line. An emergency landing was made at the same baseball complex where the private air show was held. The helicopter landed in an area between two ball fields. They landed safely, and made repairs right there. The only damage done was a minor spill of fuel which was cleaned up by the authorities. Luckily, it did not occur at a time when there could have been children in the area playing baseball.

5

DEFINING A COACH

The Manager manages the team. He or she is a coach who is assisted by additional coaches, all of whom are volunteers. After coaching Youth Baseball for seven years, I found out what the word "coach" really meant. The dictionary defines a coach as a person who trains athletes or athletic teams. The definition of "train" is, "to make proficient with specialized instruction and practice." A coach is thrown out to the wolves to fend for himself with no preparation; unlike a school teacher who attends many different courses in college to prepare to handle almost any situation. The phrase "specialized instruction" entails more than just teaching thirteen children how to play the game of baseball. I had spoken with numerous Major League managers and found out there was much more intensity at that level; and that I would be dealing with issues of both players and parents.

The coach, a teacher, is responsible for handling many situations which arise during practices and games. The coach first has to work with each player on the fundamentals of the game. That in itself is difficult enough to teach to a group of young children. The players are taught good sportsmanship, which is just as important as being taught how to play baseball. They are taught not to throw their baseball bats or baseball helmets when they are discouraged. They are told not to question an umpire's call or a coach's decision. Most important, they are told that they will win as a team, and they will lose as a team. The outcome of a game is never the fault of any one individual. The main goal is to have fun whether you win or lose, hoping that each child will develop into a good person.

A Glutton For Punishment

One of the toughest jobs for a manager is to keep a team motivated when they are having a losing season.

Coaching sounds like a fairly easy job to do, but there is much more to it than I've already mentioned. The coach has to prepare a game plan for each practice and familiarize the assistant coaches with their duties. A practice has to be presented in such a way that the ballplayers can have fun, while at the same time developing into better ball players. I always remind myself that they are just young kids, and that baseball practices should not be run like the military.

The coaches must be prepared to administer first aid if needed. A simple cut can be cleaned up and covered with a bandage, a more serious cut or scrape may need additional attention. A slight bruise is usually treated by applying an icepack to the area affected and the "imaginary injury" can be treated with a little break in the action and a confidence-building boost. The more serious injuries such as deep cuts requiring stitches, severe sprains or broken bones are what add a little stress to the coach. All coaches attend a safety meeting prior to the start of the season where they are instructed on how to handle each type of situation that may arise. This would be the extent of "specialized training" in the area of first aid.

In some communities, there could be a situation where knowledge of a second language would be necessary to communicate with an injured player on the team. Once I was at an out- of- town tournament where the players and coaches all spoke Portuguese amongst themselves. It prevented the other team from understanding anything they were saying and seemed like it was beneficial to them. Coaches in our town only needed to speak English to communicate with the players. It might be nice to learn a second language if it would be advantageous in understanding the other coach's instructions being given to his team.

A coach must also be good in science. After all, hitting a baseball at the correct time and on the correct area of the bat is a science. To teach a child who cannot hit a baseball can sometimes be quite difficult. Too many things in life are taken for granted, and not every child can be taught to hit a baseball. A player must keep his eye on the ball and see the bat hit the ball. It's a matter of good timing as to whether or not the ball is hit.

Next, a coach must be good at math. A coach has to place nine, and only nine, ball players on the ball field at one time. I've seen a coach put ten ball players on the ball field instead of nine. A coach must also keep track of balls, strikes, and outs. A coach has to make sure each player gets the required playing time in every game. The requirement, usually, is one at bat and two innings playing defense. Keeping the pitch count is another of the coach's responsibilities.

These duties, in addition to teaching the actual game of baseball are nothing compared to situations coaches are required to deal with on a daily basis. Coaches could use training in basic child psychology. Child psychology focuses on the mind and behavior of children from prenatal development through adolescence. It deals not only with how children grow physically, but with their mental, emotional, and social development as well. Most managers and coaches don't know about a ball player's home life, social life, school life or medical issues. On the child's registration form, there is a section the parents are asked to fill out regarding any medical conditions their child may have. Many parents do not wish to disclose that information, for fear their child may not be given fair consideration when being chosen for a team. What the parents don't know is the manager does not see that information until after the child has been selected. It's not right that a parent is allowed to keep a coach from being aware of a medical condition since it could create a serious problem at a later date.

The best way to get information about each player is to hold a team meeting. The parent or parents will usually speak with me after the meeting and fill me in on their child's home life, such as a mother or father not living at home or a situation involving step-parents. Sometimes I am told about a child's medical issue that was not on the registration form, yet it seems as though I always find out eventually some way or other, though not necessarily from the parents. I have found that some parents feel more comfortable speaking with one of my coaches about their child's issues. That's fine with me as long as I am eventually made aware of it.

Training on how to deal with a grieving child would also be helpful. One of the toughest jobs for a coach is to help a child deal with the death of a parent, relative or friend. I have been through this a few times and it is probably the most difficult task I've had to face.

Some training would also be nice in adult psychology, since it's not only the kids that have issues. At the team meeting I try to find out as much as I can about each child, and I also tell the parents what I expect from them. It is the coach's job to reinforce how important it is to set an example for their children. I always ask the parents to encourage the players on the team to do their best. If they make a mistake give them support, and if they make a good play or get a good hit, share the enthusiasm. The same should be true with the opposing team. Once, a grandparent from our team hollered at a player on the opposing team, saying it was his own fault that he got hit by the pitch because he didn't move out of the way. The comment was embarrassing to me, my coaches, and the parents of our team. The manager of the other team came over to everyone on our side and let them know how upset he was over the comment. The child didn't have time to move out of the way, and I wanted to crawl into a hole and hide because of the comment that was made.

Another incident which embarrassed me immensely was when one of the parents from my team got into an argument with a parent from the opposing team who was working in the concession stand. The parent from my team, who was a woman, called the other parent, also a woman, a "bimbo." Words that weren't very nice were exchanged back and forth for about five minutes. This occurred where both children and adults stood in line waiting to be served. I was informed of the altercation and was told by the President of the League to get my parents under control. I always made a point to keep my players under control at all times and never thought I would have to keep the parents in line, also.

As I said before, there is more to coaching than just teaching the game of baseball to a group of thirteen children. The actual coaching is only a small part of a coach's job. There is also more that a coach should be responsible for. Too many coaches are concerned only with the "game" and neglect to become involved with helping out the league when needed. If every coach just practiced and then played games without volunteering their services in other areas needed to run a good program, the League would not be successful. There is a lot of work that has to be done, whether by becoming involved as a member on the Board of Directors or as simple as lending a hand to keep the baseball complexes clean, keeping the fields safe to play on, or helping to maintain the equipment, buildings, and fields. There is never enough help; and unfortunately, it is usually only a small group of people who do the majority of the work.

Additionally, a coach is expected to attend the league's monthly meetings and any other special meetings that should come up which are pertinent to the running of the league. The league used to mail out a monthly newsletter to keep the players, parents, and coaches informed of what was happening in the league. Once the internet became popular, the league set up a web site which contained everything that was sent out via the newsletter and much more, with less expense. This, in a sense, can give a coach less reason to attend a monthly meeting.

6

FUNDRAISING

In addition to the ball player's yearly registration fee, additional funds are necessary to cover the expenses of the league. The first year my son played youth baseball, the league's annual fundraiser was selling M&M plain and M&M peanut candy bars. Each player was given a box of twenty-five candy bars to sell at one dollar apiece. Relatives were the likely candidates to be approached for the sale of the candy. Any candy not sold was usually bought by the child's parents. My son never successfully sold all of his candy bars, so my wife and I were always the ones to buy whatever was left. I ate the darn candy bars until they made me sick which discouraged me from eating chocolate again until the following year. The league was quite successful with the profits they made, yet the parents prayed each year that it would be the last year selling candy bars.

A few years later the Board of Directors decided to try something different. It made many parents very happy and helped them avoid putting on unwanted pounds. The new idea was to sell what was called a calendar raffle. It cost five dollars to purchase a calendar for the month of June. Each player was required to sell only five calendars. A prize of one hundred dollars was given each day during the month of June. A name was drawn every day with the winning ticket put back in for the remaining drawings, giving everyone thirty chances to win. This type of fundraiser was more profitable for the league and much healthier for all participants. Many people looked forward to the calendar raffle each year, and I never heard one person ask when we would be selling candy bars again.

There were numerous prizes given to the players who sold the most calendars. Prizes ranged from gift certificates to bicycles. It motivated the kids to sell more calendars than candy bars, since there were no prizes awarded for selling the most candy bars. I always sold fifty to sixty calendars myself to help fund the league's finances. I always told the league to pick another name if I were chosen to receive a prize. I wasn't selling them to win prizes, but there were many kids who were.

The calendar raffle raised a good amount of money, but the biggest money-maker came from the sales at the concession stand. Every year was very successful with the exception of two years. There were two individuals a few years apart from each other that were suspected of not being very honest. Sales dropped immensely during those two years with no explanation. The league implemented a new procedure that provided better accountability and sales returned to higher than normal. Available daily at the concession stand were nachos with cheese sauce, fried dough, large soft pretzels, popcorn, candy, gum, sunflower seeds, water, soda, thirst-quenching energy drinks, and a frozen slush drink with a choice of flavors. Weeknights, many players and their families lived on either steamed hotdogs or a slice or two of pizza. Sales were brisk, but Saturdays were the most profitable day since games were being played all day long. When games got rained out on Saturdays, it was tough to make up the losses, since the games were usually made up on week nights, many times at fields located on the outskirts of town which didn't have a concession stand.

On Saturdays, an outdoor grill was fired up with hotdogs, hamburgers, cheeseburgers, and Italian sausages being served. My favorite was the Italian sausage served on a fresh roll with peppers and onions. Just the smell alone would attract a crowd. Specialty items such as clam chowder, chili, or beef stew were good sellers on a cool evening in April and May. A good cup of hot coffee or hot chocolate would also warm you up at evening games.

The concession stand was tended by the players' parents. For the most part, the parents fulfilled their obligation, but occasionally a parent or two outright refused to take a turn or had excuses as to why they couldn't do it. The league depended on volunteers, yet some parents felt the league should pay someone to run the concession stand. The profits would be considerably less, and there would still be complaints. Maybe those parents that didn't want to volunteer their services would rather pay an additional twenty or twenty-five dollars a year in registration fees to cover the cost of running the league.

In addition to the fundraisers and the concession stand's profits, the league has held youth dances, adult dances, and other various fundraisers to help cover the expenses of the league. Unfortunately, vandalism and theft are ongoing problems which affect the league's treasury. A soda machine which was located outside the concession stand was smashed one night by vandals with both soda and money being stolen. Individuals have been caught numerous times breaking into the concession stands stealing money. One time it was more than money that police caught two individuals stealing. One man in his late twenties and the other in his early forties were arrested when they were found with their pockets loaded with chewing gum and slim-jims. I guess not everyone's "taste" is the same. You just never know what people are thinking.

There are many other towns which have an extended menu to choose from. I have seen items such as breakfast sandwiches, hash browns, juice, and coffee being served during morning games. Later in the day, a wide variety of items such as lobster rolls, fried chicken breast sandwiches, linguica sandwiches, cocoila – a Portuguese sandwich of seasoned pulled pork, clam chowder served in a bread bowl, chicken fingers, French fries and onion rings would be available. It was very tempting to spend a lot of money and eat a lot of food in some of those towns since the food was quite often very good. I've given more than my share of money to many of these towns while attending various all-star tournaments.

7

EVALUATIONS

It was a few weeks before tryouts were to begin, and I was looking for one or two individuals in addition to the two assistant coaches from the previous year's team who could help me evaluate the players hoping to be drafted to a Major League team. I was familiar with the process of rating the players since I had attended numerous tryouts when I was interested in coaching in the Minor League division. I would be drafting six new players to replace the six twelve-year olds that were on the previous year's team.

Until a year before, tryouts were held in March on the fields which were often still frozen and partially covered with snow. I remember a newspaper article a girl I worked with brought in one day about baseball tryouts in the early spring (actually late winter). It told how one of the boys arrived in a heavy, bulky winter coat and a pair of overshoes with metal buckles. How anyone could throw the ball or run being dressed like that seemed impossible, yet the boy did a superb job fielding and throwing the baseball, then, outran all of the other children trying out.

I suggested at one of the league meetings moving tryouts to September when the weather was still good and the kids weren't as rusty from having not thrown a baseball or hit a baseball all winter. I had also heard that other towns had tryouts in September and it worked out very well. The league agreed with me and scheduled tryouts in mid-September, not long after the kids had returned to school. It would also give the coaches an opportunity to get their teams together during the winter months to get a head-start practicing.

Finally, the week for tryouts arrived, and I had my scouts ready to take notes. Evaluations, as it was also known, were held on Monday through Thursday shortly after school got out for the day and then all day Saturday. Friday was the rain date if one of the week days got cancelled. All boys and girls ages nine through twelve were asked to attend. Each week day was assigned to a specific age group and on Saturday the eleven and twelve year olds were scheduled in the morning, then the nine and ten year olds in the afternoon.

A child had to attend at least one of the two days of evaluation in order to be eligible for the draft. Once a child was selected to play on a Major League team, he or she would automatically be on the team through his or her twelve- year- old season.

On Sunday evening, the Major League draft was held, and phone calls were made by the managers to inform the chosen players. The players not selected to play in the Major League division were not notified until the following spring when the Farm League and Minor League divisions formed their teams.

Evaluations began with each child being given a number to pin onto the back of his or her shirt. The number was used to identify each child with only a few children actually being known by name. A sheet with the player's name would eventually be handed out for future reference, but almost every coach communicated by numbers.

Individuals being evaluated were rated on various fundamentals of the game. Ground balls were hit to each child at shortstop where they fielded the ball and then made a throw to first base. Fielding and catching were observed and documented by the scouts. One year a manager videotaped the ground ball sessions so he and his coaches could review the tape at home. The next evaluation was on fly balls. The individual would track down the ball, try to make the catch, and then throw the ball in to a cutoff. The final segment was batting. A pitching machine was used to give each individual approximately twenty pitches to try to hit. The machine provided every child with the same pitch at the same speed. If an adult or two took turns pitching manually, the pitches would not be consistent and not fair to the children.

Not only did coaches and scouts learn a lot about the talent of each individual, but a lot was learned about their ability to follow instructions, their behavior while waiting their turn, and even a little bit about their parents. There were parents who coached their kids during tryouts from outside the fence, some upsetting their child and others commending their child. There were some coaches I thought who preferred not to select a child with a vocal parent while most other coaches would just set the parents straight if they were a bit too loud. There is nothing wrong with parents cheering or clapping, but coaching should be left to the coaches.

Evaluations only lasted about an hour and one half at the Monday through Thursday sessions. The groups were fairly small and it didn't take very long and only a few scouts were needed. Saturday was a different story. There were two age groups during each session and Saturday was the only day to bat. It was necessary to have additional scouts to keep up with the fast pace with three separate areas to take notes. It was literally a three-ring circus. The morning session was a little less hectic because there were only a few eleven- and twelve-year-olds. The afternoon session was always long and tiring since there were at least twice as many children as there were in the morning session. The nine- and ten-year-olds were much more energetic and it was a long afternoon for them. Sitting in a chair from 9:00 AM – 4:00 PM was a long time for a coach trying to take notes. By noontime, it started to get very warm, unlike the 4:00 PM start time on weekdays which was fairly cool. By 1:00 PM or 2:00 PM it was very easy to find yourself dozing off not only from the heat but from the hypnosis created by the repetition. If you don't catch yourself, it can be embarrassing if another coach catches you and especially if a parent outside the fence around the field catches you.

Evaluations are usually injury-free with the exception of an occasional ball which bounces up at a child's face or a ball which was thrown, but not caught in the glove, hitting the child's body. The end result was usually a swollen lip or a nice bruise which no one likes to experience. I remember one year when a ball took a bad hop hitting a nine-year-old fielder in the mouth causing him to bleed. That ended his day and his chance of being drafted to a Major League team, since he didn't return for the Saturday session to bat. He returned the following three years and finally got drafted as a twelve-year-old on a Major League team. I was the manager that drafted him, and he turned out to be a darn good fielder and one of my top three batters that year. Every year the managers remembered the incident during his nine-year-old tryout and chose not to pick him. He had a good attitude, worked very hard, and was an individual who never gave up. He was the type that started out slow as a nine-year-old, yet could develop into an All Star once he reached high school. Time will tell.

The whole process of tryouts is taken seriously by all of the Major League managers, yet a little fun is had at the same time. There's not a lot of talk about prospects since almost everyone likes to keep his thoughts a secret. When a manager is interested in a certain player, he doesn't usually let on how much he would really like to have him or her on his team. The one thing that isn't held back is when managers joke about how a certain player would be a good "Mother Pick," meaning that the mother of the child was pretty cute and it would be nice to have her as a parent on the team. Every year the comment is made and helps break up the monotony of the evaluation procedure.

Once evaluations finish on Saturday, it's time to sit down with the scouts and review notes. Everyone pretty much agrees who the top ten or twelve prospects are and figures they would be gone after the first round of the draft. The difficult task was preparing a list of names for the next fifty, sixty, or more players that would be needed to complete the draft. If a manager only needed to draft four players, he only needed to have a list of forty or fifty names. If the number of players needed was more than four, then you needed to go very deep into the list. Most of the time, once you get down to the final round it gets very tough. Trying to decide which player to select could just as well come down to a coin toss or that "Mother Pick."

I liked to carry four twelve-year-olds, four eleven-year-olds, three ten-year-olds, and two nine-year-olds on the team each year. With only four twelve-year-olds on the team, the following year I would only have to draft four new players to replace them. It meant I only had to introduce four new players into the program which meant a lot less teaching than if I had six or seven new players. The first year with my Major League team I had to replace six players which was almost half the team. It required a lot more work to familiarize them with the program. In recent years, the rules changed and required that any twelve-year-old who wanted to play in the Major League division had to be drafted onto a team. By forcing that on a manager, it changed the level of play, the opportunity to develop a good program with a fundamentally sound team, and increased the number of twelve-year-olds on most teams, therefore having to replace as many as six to eight players each year. A manager used to be able to build a team of his choice where now the league forces a manager to take an average of two to three twelve-year-olds each year who normally wouldn't have been drafted.

Sunday morning I would sit down and look over my notes again to see if I thought I had my list of choices in the correct order. Spending too much time studying each child's performance would make my head spin. After a few hours I finally put away all my notes and just waited patiently for the draft which would be held that evening. The one thing I didn't do, but had heard that some coaches did, was to get input from friends of theirs who were school teachers. It seemed like a good idea since valuable information about the children could be obtained to help out the coach. Teachers know an awful lot about the kids working with many of them or hearing about them from other teachers.

The draft was held that evening and the managers and coaches selected the players they needed to fill their roster with the mandatory thirteen players. Everyone usually seemed happy with their picks and looked forward to the beginning of another season. The next step was to call the newly drafted players to congratulate them and inform them as to which team they would be playing for.

The draft began at 7:00 PM and usually lasted until at least 9:30 PM. If the child was still up and had not already gone to bed, I asked his parents if I could speak to him and give the good news. You could tell the children were very happy and envisioned them dancing around the house when they found out they had made a Major League team. If they were not still up when I called, their parents told them the next morning.

I told the parents when I called that within a couple of weeks I would be having a pizza party to meet the new players. The party would include the players from the previous year's team and would give them a chance to meet their new teammates. The party was held at a local pizza shop which had a pool table and juke box. The kids usually devoured twelve to fifteen pizzas and drank eight to ten pitchers of soda.

The following day at school was depressing for the kids who were not chosen to play on a Major League team. The children had probably been crying at home that morning when they found out they hadn't received a phone call informing them they had made a Major League team. There was always an issue when a nine-year-old had made a team yet a ten-, eleven- or especially a twelve-year-old had not. It was difficult for the children to understand the reasoning behind it and even more difficult for the parents. Once the rule that guaranteed all twelve-year-olds would be chosen to play in the Major League was implemented, most of the complaining stopped.

Each team usually drafted one or two nine-year-olds since they were the best players from that age group. It takes a year or two for a player to develop and adjust to the Major League program. By the time they reach eleven or twelve years old they are usually at their prime. The parents of children that weren't chosen to play in the Major League division didn't understand the reasoning and frequently took it out on the managers and coaches. I myself have been questioned many times by parents, and I've tried explaining to them the best I can the logic behind it.

Sometimes trying to teach a first year twelve-year-old is like trying to teach a first year nine-year-old. There is just not enough time to teach that twelve-year-old everything he or she needs to know in only a few weeks. The nine-year-old will have much more time to develop and is expected to take longer.

I have nothing against a twelve-year-old child who would like to play in the Major League division, but in most cases they would probably be happier playing in the Minor League division which is the level where many of them belong. More than likely, they would get more playing time and have more fun. If I were that twelve-year-old, I would prefer to play as many innings as I could play at the level where I belonged, since playing beats sitting on the bench. A child has to learn that life isn't always going to be perfect. A twelve-year-old who is going to be guaranteed they will make a Major League team is comparable to the individual that gets promoted to a job because they have a connection by knowing the right person instead of having the required skills or being best qualified. Children have to learn sooner or later that it takes hard work to move on in life.

There have been some embarrassing and upsetting events that occurred over the years at the draft. I was embarrassed when I selected a player who had not attended tryouts. The managers started hollering at me and said I couldn't select the child. Come to find out, one of my coaches who had attended the tryouts to help me scout, had given the player high ratings only because he had coached him the previous year in Farm League and knew his capabilities. I didn't have any ratings on the child and thought I just might have missed him trying out, so I went along with my coach's advice. The following year, the child did try out, and I selected him fair and square.

Another year, a manager was given the wrong paper work and phone number of a player he had selected. The manager only looked at the last name and called to inform the child he was selected and to congratulate him. The manager found out the next day he had spoken with the wrong child and his parents, so the President of the league had to resolve the matter. Eventually, the manager did get the correct player on his team.

One of the most frustrating situations happened to another manager when he selected a player for his team. The manager had placed a different child's ratings on his sheet beside the player he selected. The manager thought he was choosing a fairly decent nine-year-old, but in all actuality the child was not very talented at all. There was no way to resolve the problem, therefore, the manager was forced to carry the player on his team for four years.

8

THE MAJOR LEAGUE – MY FIRST YEAR

Being chosen to play on a Major League team is the goal of almost every child who wants to play baseball. Many days and years of practice can fulfill that child's dream. In many cases, a coach's child excels above most other players. The reason is that many of those coaches spend a lot of time working with their child, where other parents don't spend as much time with theirs. This is true in any sport and it only makes sense. Many times, parents of the other children on the team feel that the coach's child gets more playing time only because of the relationship. Once in a while that may be the case, but nine out of ten times the child is further advanced.

My first day as a Major League coach, I was asked by a few parents if I had a child playing on the team. My answer was no, and I told them my son had finished playing in the league the previous year. I told them I had no more children who would be playing youth baseball, and that I decided to continue coaching because I loved the game. I'm sure the reason I was asked was because parents were curious if I would be one of those coaches who would favor his child over theirs. I thought, for that reason, it was very important to inform the parents.

I had called for a practice a few days after the draft, since I was excited about meeting my new team. There were the seven returning players from the previous year's team and the six new players I had just drafted. Even though the managers were told not to hold practices until January 1st, I ignored the rule. It was not a good way to start out my new career as a

Major League manager, but I was anxious to get a look at the team. I had seen the six players I had drafted during evaluations, but I had not seen the other seven players either as a person or a player. The first get-together went pretty well as most of the team showed up. I found out a lot about the veterans who were there and got to put names in place of numbers to my six new draftees. I couldn't wait for winter to pass so I could get back outside to practice.

March finally arrived and the baseball fields were just about clear from the winter's snow. They were almost dry enough to practice on when an unexpected snow storm decided to drop about eight inches of snow on April 1st. What an April Fools' Day joke had been put on me as a new Major League manager. It would have been a late start due to a long winter as it was, but now I was forced to wait even longer to hold my first practice. I was so anxious to get started I didn't care about the snow, so I scheduled the team to meet at the school parking lot, next to the baseball fields, which had been plowed. The temperature wasn't that cold, and I didn't care that we would be playing on the pavement.

The parking lot worked out pretty well, since it was large enough to hit both ground balls and fly balls to the kids. The parents must have thought I was crazy, but I was excited just as much as the nine-year-olds that had made the team. The pavement made a mess of the baseballs from all of the scuffing, yet I really didn't care because I finally had my first outdoor get-together with the whole team.

The snow melted very quickly, and we were able to hold a real practice on the baseball field within a week. There was not a lot of time for any team to prepare for the first game of the season which was only a week away. Somehow, all of the teams would have to get their players ready for the first game.

My two assistant coaches, who had helped me during tryouts, each had a child returning to the team. I asked them if they would continue to assist me during the season, since I knew they had experience coaching in the Major League division. They both agreed to help out, and I was very happy, as were they.

Returning to the team were three cousins. One of them was the ten-year-old son of one of my assistant coaches, and the other two were eleven-years-olds. The previous manager of the team, for whom I had taken over, had a son on the team who was also a cousin to the three cousins on my team but had completed his twelve-year-old season the previous year. I was prepared for a scenario of competitiveness amongst the three I had returning and could only imagine what it must have been like with a fourth on the team. After our first real outdoor practice, I was right about the competitiveness. I had inherited the team, so I just did the best I could. I knew from the previous years that brothers were usually competitive, although sometimes there were never any issues. Sometimes parents even requested that a brother or sister play on different teams.

A coach with a child on his team had a tendency to be tougher on his child than the other players. I was tougher on my son in any sport that he played where I coached him, only because he thought he could get away with doing what he wanted, and not because I was pushing him to do better, as most of the coaches with a child on the team would do. When I had a coach like that, I would ask him not to "coach" only his child, but to focus more on the other players on the team and I would offer instruction to his child. There was a lot less pressure on the child that way, and the kids seemed more relaxed with less stress caused by the parent.

I noticed the biggest difference in the way a child performed, especially when pitching, was when the parent, whether coaching or as a spectator, kept quiet. It is difficult enough for a child to pitch in a game without the constant guidance being given by any coach. Even a parent watching the game as a spectator distracts the child by constantly shouting instructions from the sideline between each pitch. It would be better if all parents just sat back, kept quiet, and enjoyed the game. It would be best if the parents weren't there at all. Since that would never happen, applauding at the end of each inning would be sufficient.

There have been a few occasions when I have had children pitch a game in which either their parent, a coach, or spectator were not at the game or where both parents were not at the game. The end result was that the children all pitched excellent games with it being obvious they were much more relaxed and not under as much pressure as when their parents were there.

My first year was a bit challenging. It was a rebuilding year with six new players which, in all actuality, was almost half of the team. We won our first game of the season, which got us off to a good start. The kids worked hard all year long, learned a lot about baseball, and never gave up. I also learned a lot. Our record was 8-14 for the year, which was better than I expected it would be. In the off-season, I put together a little better program and became better organized. All in all, I was pretty excited and looking forward to my second season.

This was also the year that led to my addiction to sunflower seeds. I only partook during games, not during practices. The process was simple. Step 1: Crack the shell with your teeth. Step 2: Eat the seed and spit out the shell. End Result: Relief of stress caused by the ball players. Once I got good at it, I could put a handful of seeds in my mouth and store them in one corner like a squirrel, then, I would transfer a seed over to the other side with my tongue, crack it, then eat the seed and spit out the shell. It became a ritual that I continued during every game, thereafter. I can think of many worse habits that I could have picked up and consider my addiction to sunflower seeds as minute.

9

PUTTING TOGETHER A PROGRAM

The following year after tryouts, I heard that some of the managers took their players to an indoor batting cage during the winter months to work on their hitting. There also was a manager who rented one of the school gymnasiums from the middle of January until the weather was good enough to practice outdoors. They met once a week for two hours and worked on the fundamentals of the game. I thought that would be a good idea for my team sometime, but I heard about a facility that had batting cages, pitching mounds and a set up for soft toss. Soft toss was a drill where a baseball was tossed from about four feet away from the side of a batter to a spot where it could be hit by the batter into a fence, screen or wall roughly six feet in front of the batter. Each player was given approximately twenty-five or thirty balls to hit. It was a good way to loosen up the batter and practice the timing of his swing. It was a very simple drill, and it only took a few minutes for each child to complete. For two hours, the cost was quite reasonable and for a few dollars more we could use a basketball court in the same facility which had a hard rubber floor which was ideal for hitting ground balls for the players to field and make throws like in a game. I rented the facility and accomplished a lot indoors for a few years until the cost to rent the facility sky-rocketed and the opportunity came about to use the same school gymnasium the other manager had been renting which was a lot less expensive.

Unlike the first facility I had rented, the gymnasium was less hectic and I could take more time to work on various drills without being rushed.

It was a great way for me and my coaches to get to know the kids and give the kids a chance to meet each other. It was an opportunity for the kids to start working together as a team prior to outdoor practices. The kids loved it because they got the feeling they were at Spring Training just like the professional baseball players, especially when it was snowing outside. It helped condition the players since there are not too many weeks of good weather to practice outside prior to Opening Day which is usually towards the middle of April.

When we practiced indoors, we always had to use tee balls so the floor of the gymnasium did not get ruined by a regular baseball. A baseball could scratch the finish on the floor, break windows or damage other objects in the gymnasium. A baseball could also possibly injure a player or coach since everyone is so close to each other inside a small gymnasium compared to a large area like a baseball field.

There were many throwing, catching, and fielding drills that the players could work on indoors. After a few weeks, once the kids had been throwing and their arms became stronger, I started to work with those who would be pitching and catching. Everyone was given a chance to try pitching, yet not every child that plays baseball is meant to be a pitcher. Until everyone's arms were in good shape, there were many fundamentals that could be worked on. One of the drills the players did over and over was catching the baseball as though they were taking a cut-off and then learning how they should turn and throw the baseball to the next player who would make the play as though it were a game situation. The player who was the cut-off was taught to stand sideways with his glove-side closest to the person to whom he would throw the ball. After catching the baseball, the player was to turn as quickly as possible, taking a step forward while releasing the ball. For some reason, many of them would turn the wrong way which in turn wasted valuable time getting the ball to its destination. It was not only the nine-year-old who would turn the wrong way, but the twelve-year-olds, also. Some twelve-year-olds never learned even by the end of the season. What was astonishing to me was the nine-year-old who joined the team a few games into the season, attending his first practice and understanding exactly what to do the first time I explained it to him. I had him go through the drill a few times, and he did every step perfectly. I asked if he knew why he should turn to his glove-side, and his response shocked me. He told me that turning one-hundred-eighty degrees was a shorter turn than three-hundred-sixty degrees. Therefore, he could get the ball quicker to its destination by turning towards his glove-side. It was not the type of answer that I or anyone would expect to come from a nine year old child. Every time he caught the baseball thereafter, he turned the correct way and threw the baseball as he had been instructed.

The kids performed various batting drills such as hitting off a baseball tee, soft toss, and bunting. They always questioned me why they were using a baseball tee at this level because they thought a tee was used only by the younger kids in tee ball. I explained that even professional baseball players practice hitting off a tee since it makes them keep their eyes focused on the baseball which is an important aspect of batting.

Aside from throwing, catching, fielding, and batting, the team was instructed on the proper way to run the bases. They were taught how to "belly out" meaning how to take a wide turn prior to touching first base if there was a chance they would be continuing to second base on a well-hit ball into the outfield. They were taught how and when to steal bases along with the procedure to follow should a base runner get caught in a rundown. The practices ended with running races one-on-one and then relay races. The running gave me a good idea how fast each player could run should I decide to keep him running for an additional base in a game, and it also helped me determine where the players could best be placed on the field defensively.

Working on these various drills indoors gave the team more time to work on the things impossible to do indoors once they got outside. Since there is so little time to practice outside prior to the start of the season, it is nice to have access to an indoor facility. The indoor batting cages become more popular every year, but it's very expensive for the amount of time each player gets to bat when there are thirteen players all waiting to take a turn. Unless the child's parents take them on their own, to me it doesn't seem worthwhile. Pre-season practice has become popular with many of the teams in the Major League division. What started out with one or two teams has grown to all but two or three teams practicing out of the twelve teams in the Major League division. Our town is known as a baseball town and the familiar phrase "Play Ball" can't come soon enough.

Also in the gymnasium, I hold the team/parent meeting where I explain to the players and the parents what I expect from each of them during the season. It's a lot more involved than what I expected from a tee ball team. I always start off by addressing the rules of playing time as well as the rules of pitching. The rules of playing time are very simple. The rule states that every player must get one time at bat and play defensively for a minimum of six consecutive outs. Only a player in the starting line-up who has been removed for a substitute may re-enter the game once, in any position in the batting order provided his or her substitute has fulfilled the required time at bat and defensive play. The rules of pitching are also very simple. The rule states that a player who pitched in less than four innings is required one calendar day of rest before pitching again, and a player who pitched in four or more innings is required three calendar days of rest before pitching again. This pitching rule remained in effect until two years ago when the league introduced a pitch count rule which limited the number of pitches a pitcher could throw in a game, then requiring a determined number of days rest depending on the pitcher's age and the number of pitches the pitcher had thrown. This was beneficial to the pitcher, since many young baseball players ruined their arms by throwing too many pitches at such a young age. I always tell the players who will be the starting pitcher of the next game. The reason I do is so they don't come to the game tired from not getting enough sleep the previous night, and so they don't overdue in their activities during the day if the game is not in the morning. This pertains mostly to Saturday games. Most important, I tell them not to practice pitching with a friend or parent on the day of the game they are scheduled to pitch, since it will only tire out their arm. I've had players pitching in a game tell me after two or three innings their arms were getting tired only because they had pitched a half a games worth of pitches in their back yard prior to the game.'

I stress that what determines ones playing time is not his age but how hard one works in practices, and what the end result shows to the coaches. A perfect example was when the mother of a twelve-year-old complained to me after a game that she was upset that her son didn't start in the game that day. I said that he had missed the last five practices, and it was not a good example to set for his teammates by starting him. His mother had told me earlier in the season that he might miss a few practices because he had to be home for his younger brother and sister when they got home from school. I thought a few would be acceptable due to the circumstances, but when I went home that evening and checked his attendance records, I found that he had made only two of the previous ten practices. He was one who never attended the optional Sunday practices only because he had better things to do. By coming to a Sunday practice, it would have shown me that at least he was coming to practice whenever possible. I felt I did the right thing.

Whenever I asked a team if winning regular season games, playoff games, or championship games was more important to them than getting equal playing time, the majority preferred to win games. After all, isn't that the object of playing games in any sport, to win? Many times it's the parents who are unhappy about their child's playing time and not the kids. The reason for having coaches is to teach the game of baseball and learn how not only to win games but also learn how to accept losing games. I stress to the players on my teams, you win as a team and you lose as a team. Win or lose, they should have fun. Any parent can take a group of children to a ball field and pick up teams to play a game for the purpose of having fun. If the parents prefer doing that, maybe they will end up getting a taste of how to handle playing time, if there are thirteen players on each team. It may be easy since there would be no reward for winning games.

The first issue I address involving safety, is that no jewelry should be worn during practices or games with the exception of a bracelet or necklace noting that the child has a medical condition of some sort. Major League Baseball professionals only make matters worse by wearing their thick gold chains which even for them could create a safety issue with the chance of being choked, causing youth baseball players to wonder why they can't wear theirs. I next address what I consider the most important rule concerning everyone's safety. Every child possesses a weapon, which is simply the baseball bat. My rule is very simple, yet I always have to remind every player more than once during the season. A baseball bat is only to be swung when a batter is in the batter's box during batting practice, during a game, or with the coach while the batter is hitting the ball, while hitting soft toss, or off the tee. I have seen children hit by a baseball bat by another child not paying attention while swinging the bat. I have had numerous close calls myself from players not paying attention to their surroundings. The other rule regarding baseball bats is when a child during a game hits the baseball, he must drop the bat prior to running and not throw the bat with the chance of hitting the catcher or home plate umpire.

The next topic I discuss is behavior. There are many areas which I have to address. What bothers me the most, I tell them, is when a player either strikes out swinging or is called out on strikes by the home plate umpire and the batter pounds his bat on home plate and then again on the ground repeatedly while walking back to the dugout. I also demand they do not throw their batting helmet or baseball bat on the ground once they get off the field. They are also told never to complain or argue with the umpire, manager, or coaches when they disagree with a call. Even showing signs of displeasure from their facial expressions upsets an umpire and coaches. Most importantly, they are told they should never swear.

I also explain to them that when choosing nicknames for their teammates, it should be agreed upon with the player before being used. Bad-mouthing teammates and keeping their hands to themselves is also addressed. I'm adamant that there is no trash talking to the other team either on the field or at school. I ask that they pay attention, work hard, listen to the coaches, and not horse around. I next tell the veteran twelve-year-olds on the team they are now the leaders of the team, and they should set a good example for the younger players and any new twelve-year-old players on the team. One year there were two twelve-year-olds who brought a yo-yo and a super ball to a game which caused a distraction in the dugout. That ended very quickly once I confiscated the toys. I stress that a lot can be learned just by watching the veterans who are considered by me as being teachers to the rookies as much as the coaches are. I can't tell them enough times how important it is to attend practices, and I ask them to inform me should they have a good reason as to why they can't make a practice. I let them know that their school work is more important than baseball, and that I would appreciate if they would let me know if they were having problems with their school work, and if so I would have no problem with them coming late or missing a practice if they needed extra help after school. Over the course of the season, I always check with each child to make sure everything is going well in school.

Next is a rule I expect every player to follow. It's a plain and simple rule which involves food and drinks. I stress that only candy, gum, sunflower seeds, water, soda, thirst-quenching energy drinks, or the fruit flavored frozen slush is allowed in the dugout during games. I ask that the parents purchase such items during the game for their child, so the child does not have to leave the dugout. The only time I allow a child to leave is when they request to use the bathroom, after notifying a coach. The players should always stay in the dugout and be ready to play should they be called upon.

I ask the parents to feed their children before or after the game and not during a game. I've had a child bring a hamburger, an order of French fries and a soft drink from the local burger joint into the dugout during a game and proceed to eat it in front of his teammates. There was also a player who decided to bring two slices of pizza and a basket of nachos and cheese sauce into the dugout during a game. There was even a player once that left the dugout without asking and bought a hotdog and soft drink and proceeded to sit in the bleachers with his mother during the game. After these incidents and a couple of other incidents, I had to address the situation prior to the start of each season. Finally, the veterans on the team couldn't wait to remind me and my coaches that it was the rookies' responsibility to carry the baseball gear to a practice or a game from my truck to the dugout and back to the truck after the practice or game. I also told the players that it didn't have to be the rookies that carried all of the equipment, but anyone could help out. I said by doing that, they could earn some "brownie points", meaning I would recognize them for their extra effort. One of the boys on the team went home and asked his mother what I meant, wondering if I was making reference to him since his skin color was brownish-black. His mother explained to him what I meant, and when she told me the next day, she and I both laughed.

Before I addressed the parents with my final comments, I gave my coaches the opportunity to say a few words to the players. Once they finished, I ended my portion of the meeting, stressing not only to the parents but also to the coaches, how important it was for them, like the children to control themselves from unnecessary outbursts during a game. I asked them to spread the word to all family members and friends who would be attending the games. I told them that if there were any issues regarding any of my players or parents, I would be the one that would be brought in front of the Board of Directors. It would usually be the individuals that weren't in attendance for the pre-season meeting that caused the problems or complained about the issues I had addressed at the meeting. I ended the meeting asking if anyone had any questions before I turned the meeting over to my "Team Mother."

Prior to the inception of a "Team Mother," the manager of the team was responsible for handling the day to day operation of the team. The position of a "Team Mother" has only been in existence for the past six years. A "Team Mother" assists the manager with duties outside of coaching. She is usually the mother of a child on the team who volunteers her services. There have been "Team Mothers," who were the manager's wife who did not have any children on the team. She pulls out the team's practice schedule and game schedule from the master schedules, prints them up and distributes them to each player. She gives out information regarding the yearly fundraisers, hands out the schedule for "Picture Day", and makes phone calls to the players if a practice has been canceled or a game postponed. Assisting a manager with these little projects and anything else along the way gives a manager more time to focus on baseball and less time to worry about the secretarial duties.

The "Team Mother's" most difficult assignment is soliciting parents for field preparation and concession duties. The visiting team of a game is responsible for preparing the field before a game, which includes raking the infield, the baselines, the area around home base and the pitcher's mound. Marking lime is then used to line the baselines and the batter's box. The home team is responsible for staffing the concession stand during the game. Usually, it's the fathers who volunteer to prep the fields and the mothers that volunteer to work in the concession stand. Each parent is asked to sign up to volunteer twice during the season for each of the duties. It's not unusual to have the volunteers that signed up for their turn somehow forget their commitment. The coaches would have to take time away from the pre-game warm-ups of the players to prepare the field, or a mother or father would have to fill in to take the place of the missing concession worker. This made it unfair because a parent would have concession duty on three different occasions unless the other individual took one of the replacements other days.

Towards the end of the season, the "Team Mother" handed out information regarding All-Star teams and tryouts, coordinated the end of the season team cookout and the planning of a trip to see a local professional baseball game. The team was a member within an Association of Professional Baseball, yet not affiliated with "Major League Baseball." It was a fun night out for my team with the opportunity to get signed autographs from the players and the thrill of running on to the field with the players to positions they themselves played during the year. The children's names were announced over the public address system along with the players of the starting lineup for that evening's game. Once the game started, the players on my team enjoyed having their share of food, drink, and souvenirs. A good time was had by the kids and their families, even though it usually fell on a school night which would keep the kids up later than normal. I appreciated all the time my "Team Mother" devoted to the team, and without her assistance over the course of the season I don't know what I would have done. The job she did was as important as the job the coaches did assisting me.

Once my "Team Mother" had addressed everything on her list, I handed over the distribution of uniforms to any of the mothers that were willing to handle the fittings of the uniforms. Unlike in the Tee Ball through the Minor League divisions where only a tee shirt with the team name and number along with a hat were given to each player which they could keep at the end of the season, the players in the Major League division were assigned a full uniform which was returned at the end of the season and passed on from year to year. The players were told the only time they could wear their uniforms was during a game and nowhere else. I remember the year my son made his Major League team, and the day he received his uniform. The uniforms were handed out one evening at the conclusion of his outdoor practice. The players were trying on uniforms in the concession stand or in their parent's cars. It was getting dark and there was mass confusion. I thought that handing out the uniforms indoors where it was warm, well-lit and a locker room available for cleanliness and privacy would be a much better idea. I had the shirts on hangers separated by sizes as well as the pants which were not on hangers yet folded neatly in piles according to size. From that point on, it was up to the mothers to fit each child with the proper size uniform. I found that when I tried to do it myself, I was ready to pull out my hair. Women do a much better job.

It was the nine-year-old who cherished the uniform the most. He couldn't wait to put on the uniform for Opening Day. Parents have told me their child slept in the uniform the night before Opening Day because they were so excited. It was also the nine-year-old that looked forward to Picture Day, to have their picture taken for a magazine cover, their own personal baseball card or the team picture. The Team Picture is the most memorable, since it provides a lasting memory of their first year as a Major League player. There are only fourteen uniforms for my team and thirteen players. There isn't much choice for a player wanting a certain jersey number. The only way to hand out jerseys is to line up the players by height starting with the shortest players first. Not many players can keep their favorite number for all four years. Almost every player grows from year to year, therefore having to get a different size jersey and number. Only a handful of players in my thirteen years have been able to keep the same number. One player thought he could wear the same number a second year even though the jersey was skin-tight. I reminded him he would need room for not only a bead of sweat but an additional undergarment to keep warm on one of the many cool days or nights that we were guaranteed to have during the season. After a little persuasion by his parents, he agreed to take a larger jersey with a different number.

10

Practice Makes Perfect

Years ago when I was a child there were not as many activities available to choose from as there are nowadays. The local Y.M.C.A. held various indoor programs for the children in town twelve months of the year. During the spring and into the summer, the Youth Baseball League, which was equivalent to today's Major League division existed but with only eight teams. During the summer, the town's Park Department provided a baseball program week days in the morning at the local playground. The only problem was it was limited to ten-, eleven- and twelve-year-olds. It didn't allow many children to play baseball, but it was better than nothing. If any other children in town wanted to play baseball, they had to play at home or in an open field. There was the Sunday School Basketball League which was available for children from the ages of ten to eighteen years old during the winter months, but only if the child attended religious programs. The only other activities for children, as I recall, were Cub Scouts and Boy Scouts for boys and Brownies and Girl Scouts for the girls. Nowadays there is also soccer, football, hockey, softball, and soon to be, lacrosse, in our town. There are also a variety of self-defense classes and dance and cheerleading classes only to name a few of the activities available for children. Within the last few years, the Youth Baseball League has also added a Fall Ball program.

In addition to all of the local sports and activities previously mentioned, there are opportunities to compete as amateur athletes in programs that are run in addition to many of the town's athletic programs. To add even more to a child's busy schedule, camps are available for children to attend in most sports prior to or at the conclusion of the sport's regular season. With all of these opportunities, unfortunately for the baseball manager like me, many children choose to participate in more than one activity at a time, therefore causing a child to miss an occasional practice or game. I feel as though the kids get burnt out, even though their parents claim that their child likes keeping busy. With the high cost of college tuitions, it seems as though the parents hope their children will succeed in sports at a level in which they will receive a four-year scholarship.

What bothers me most, though, is when the parents neglect to share that information with me in advance about a conflict. I've dealt with it the best I could without causing a big scene, where some managers get into it with their parents of players on their team causing major problems. Spring soccer was the activity which conflicted most with baseball. The child that had back-to-back practices or games was usually dragging by the time he arrived for the second activity. Unfortunately, baseball was usually the second activity.

The Major League division is not like Tee Ball or any other division in between. A player must be devoted to the team and attend all practices. Baseball is taken seriously at this level, and if a child does not want to take on the responsibility, he should consider playing in the Farm League or Minor League division. There are many children who were not chosen to play in the Major League division, yet would be willing to devote themselves to the game they love if only given the opportunity. It's unfortunate that many children are forced by their parents to try out for the Major League when the child would prefer to play at a lower level, which would require less practice, or maybe not even play baseball at all.

I expected my team to attend the week-day practices when scheduled. I would ask them to arrive fifteen minutes prior to when we could actually take the field for practice. That way they could loosen up and be ready to go once we got on the ball field. It never seemed to work out since there were always some players that didn't show up until practice had started. The reason I was given for a child being late was that the parents were unable to get the child there on time because of the parent's busy schedule. I even offered their child a ride, if needed, but they usually refused the ride. There wasn't much I could say, but I kept trying to get the players there on time.

Every year, there was at least one player who arrived for practice at least a half hour early. You could tell they were the ones who loved the game of baseball. I was always there before they arrived, either preparing the field for practice, if there was not another team practicing before us, or waiting for a practice to end. I wished that the rest of the team were dedicated only half as much as the early birds. The players that arrived early were also the ones who stayed around after practice to continue playing with a friend if there was not another team practicing or a game scheduled on the field. On the other end of the spectrum, it was the same players that arrived fifteen or twenty minutes late for practice, that asked to be excused fifteen or twenty minutes before the practice was scheduled to end.

I enjoyed talking and working with the team at practices. After a day's work, I looked forward to hitting baseballs to them whether it were ground balls or fly balls. It gave me a chance to release stored up energy or frustration from the day. I had a favorite bat that I used which gave me complete control of wherever I wanted to hit the ball. I also loved the ping sound it made when I hit the ball. Due to my mistake, I left the bat with one of my coaches to use at a practice which I was unable to attend. The next day when I went through the bag of equipment, the bat was nowhere to be found. I asked the coach if he had it and he told me he thought he put it away with the equipment. I never found the bat, and I was devastated. It reminded me of when I was a small child of about six years old and I lost my favorite professional baseball team hat when I went on vacation. After searching high and low and even making numerous phone calls out of state to where we vacationed, my parents were unable to locate my hat. For years I thought about that hat which was never to be found. At the end of the season, one of the parents of a player on my team who had just completed his final year of Youth Baseball gave me a fungo bat as a gift to use for practices. It was a nice bat, but it was just not the same.

Practices usually lasted an hour and one-half and began with the players playing catch with one another, to loosen up their arms. Once the team had finished, it was time to do stretching exercises followed by the running of a lap around the inside perimeter of the ball field. I usually spoke with the team before we started any drills, to explain what we would be doing that day for practice. The first drill we did at every practice is what I called "Around the Horn". The players took a spot on each of the four bases and were supposed to throw the ball from home base, to first base, to second base, the third base, and then back to home base. The players took turns on a rotating basis, so each of them got involved. The object was to make good throws and good catches, with the goal being ten successful cycles around the bases without dropping the ball. It sounded pretty simple, but many times I stopped the drill before reaching the goal due to time constraints.

There were three different types of practices that I ran. The first option was hitting ground balls to the infielders and fly balls to the outfielders with the players rotating so everyone had the opportunity to field the ball in each area. After a good session of fielding, the players each took a turn hitting soft toss, followed by a turn of batting practice.

The second option was placing nine players in each position on the field with the remaining four players being base runners. I would hit balls in what was called game situations. The fielders had to make the correct play and the runners were to listen to the coaches at first and third base as they would during a regular game. It was good practice for both the offense and defense. The players rotated fielding and base running until everyone had had a turn. The second half of practice, the players had a brief batting practice.

The third option was what every player wanted to do at every practice. The players split up into two teams and had a scrimmage. One of the coaches pitched with an additional coach or two filling the vacant outfield positions. Whenever we had a batting practice or scrimmage, I usually used the coaches to pitch and not the players. A scrimmage was good once in a while to help break up the routine of drills.

During any of these practices, the kids had a little game of their own they played which was targeted at me. Whether I was pitching or hitting baseballs to them, as they returned the balls to me they would try to hit my cup of hot coffee or iced coffee which I had placed on the ground beside me. Kidding with them, I told them if they knocked over my drink they would be dead meat. Occasionally they did knock over my drink, but lived to tell about it.

There was a fun little game we occasionally played at the end of practice, which the kids really enjoyed. One at a time, I would hit each player a fly ball in center field which they were supposed to catch and then throw the ball into a rubbish barrel which I had laid down on its side behind home base with the opening directly in line with center field. Only one or two players were successful each time, yet all of the players had a lot of fun cheering on each other as their throws were heading towards the barrel.

Sunday practices were not mandatory. Sunday school or other church activities took precedence. The League determined that a manager could not hold it against a player if he did not attend the practice. All I did on Sundays was batting practice, and it was beneficial for those players who were struggling with their batting. Since it wasn't mandatory, there were players without religious obligations who chose to stay home and play video games or some other activity instead of attending practice. Those that attended often worked their way into more playing time, since they had improved their hitting. I didn't care if only three players showed up for a Sunday practice, I was still willing to help them better themselves with their hitting.

Birthday parties were the most common reason for not being able to attend a Sunday practice. Once in a while there was some other type of function given as the reason. It was usually a different child each week who had an obligation, which to me was not a problem. One year there was a player on a team that could have used batting practice more than any other member on the team. Four weeks in a row, the player could not attend practice because he had four different First Communions to attend, followed by a party. It seemed a bit out of the ordinary, but I didn't question his religious involvement. It reminded me of a co-worker friend of mine who missed numerous days of work due to the death of his grandmother. With every new supervisor we had, my friend needed to take a day off for a funeral of his mother's mother. Before my friend took a job at another one of our offices, I believe he had buried the same grandmother four or five times. Since he left for his new job, I wouldn't be surprised if he had buried her at least two or three more times.

When the practices ended, most parents arrived ahead of time and were waiting to pick up their children. I had a quick talk in the dugout with the players about the practice and our next time together. On a very hot day, it was common for one of the player's parents to treat the team to a frozen juice bar or an ice cream bar. I always had to remind them to take all of their belongings since there was always at least one player leaving something behind. They were always in a big hurry to leave to go home. By the time I made a final check around the dugout for articles that might have been left behind, it was usually too late to catch the forgetful one before he had driven away. One year I had a player that who left a different item each day. I found his baseball glove, his backpack with his school books, his sweatshirt, and his jacket. Sometimes he left the same articles more than once, but he never forgot his two-hundred dollar baseball bat. Even after numerous trips to his house with his forgotten belongings and a constant reminder every day after practices, he still seemed to leave something behind. It was a long four years with him on the team and many gallons of gas used to return his belongings.

If a parent told me ahead of time that he would be running a few minutes late, I didn't mind and I would stay with the child until he arrived. There always seemed to be one or two parents who expected babysitting service without the courtesy of calling me on my cell phone to let me know they were running late. I understood that once in a while there would be an exception, yet some parents thought that a manager had nothing better to do than sit around an extra fifteen minutes waiting for them to arrive. I always asked one of my coaches to stay with me, so I wouldn't be alone with the child. Every manager and coach has to protect themselves from possible accusations against them. I especially felt uncomfortable when a parent asked me if I could give their child a ride home from a practice or a game. When I was coaching in the Minor League division, I was asked to bring home two twelve-year-old girls on my team after practice. I probably wouldn't have agreed except that one of the girls was the daughter of one of my coaches who couldn't make the practice and the other girl was the daughter of my wife's friend whom she worked with and knew me personally. It was still a bit uncomfortable, but I brought them home without any problems.

The one incident that upset me the most was after a pre-season practice at a local school gymnasium. I stayed with one of my players for almost thirty minutes waiting for his mother to pick him up. I tried contacting her on her cell phone with no luck, and her son was getting quite upset. When his mother finally arrived, she apologized to me and said she had gotten "tied up" in the grocery store. I told her I wouldn't have minded waiting with her son for a few minutes in an emergency situation, but it would have been appreciated if she had given me a phone call. She said she would try not to let it happen again, yet she really didn't act like it was that big a deal. I never blew up at any of the parents, but there were times I came close. I'm sure if they were in my shoes it would be different. There's not much a manager can do but to bite his tongue. That's one reason why they call me, a man at 6'6" tall, "The Gentle Giant."

11

Who's On First?

With my Major League team, I did the same thing I had done in the Minor League Division on the first day of practice. I ran the practice like it was a tryout. My coaches and I had to determine what position or positions a player was capable of playing. At this first practice, there were times when my coaches and I would look at each other and question what we saw in one of our newly drafted players after watching them on the ball field. Sometimes a child has an excellent tryout, but when practices actually begin, they don't do as well. It only took a few practices to evaluate the team and from there on it would be time to start teaching the players their responsibilities of the position we felt they would do best at. There are some children that are natural ball players who are comfortable and knowledgeable players no matter where you put them.

Pitchers and catchers are usually twelve-year-olds, since it takes time for both of them to develop. During practices, I like to give all of the players on the team an opportunity to both pitch and catch. Since time constraints allowed only a few of players to take a turn during each practice, the players usually ended up having only two or three sessions during the season's practices to be worked with.

The pitcher on a team is pretty much in charge of the game. The pitcher controls the pace of the game and is the individual that can dominate a game. A strong pitcher that strikes out ten or twelve batters a game gives the defensive players very little to do. With only a minimal number of runs being scored by their teammates, pitchers can usually cruise right along without a lot of pressure on them. There are many twelve-year-olds who would love to be pitchers, yet are just not meant to be. Because they don't pitch doesn't mean they are failures, and trying to get parents to understand that is sometimes quite difficult. I have had years when a nine- or ten-year-old came in to pitch in relief who were capable of pitching an inning or two while earning a save.

The catcher is the second most important player on the team. The catcher very often is the reason a pitcher can win games. A catcher must be able to communicate to the other defensive players instructing them on what to do prior to when a batter steps up to the plate. They must also keep an eye on every base runner, being ready to make a strong and accurate throw in the event a base runner tries to steal a base. Most importantly, they must be capable of stopping balls thrown in the dirt and balls thrown either high or outside of a batter. The worst nightmare for a manager is when the catcher allows a ball to get by him with runners on base. It's bad enough for a base runner on first or second base to advance to second or third base respectively, but when a base runner on third base is allowed to score, more often than not it is that run that can make the difference in winning or losing the game. Believe it or not, some of the best catchers I've seen were girls.

Whenever I ask players on my team if they would like to try catching during a practice, most of them show little or no interest. Even when I explain that a catcher is usually guaranteed to play all six innings of a game, they still are usually not interested. It may be the many responsibilities of a catcher which scares them away. Many games in youth baseball are lost due to defensive mistakes, not only by the catcher, but by their teammates. I use the term "we beat ourselves," when the team as a whole made numerous mistakes which caused the team to lose. At first, the kids didn't understand the statement until I explained a little more thoroughly.

The first baseman is also usually a twelve-year-old, who is capable of catching a hard thrown ball. Not only does the player have to handle good throws, he also has to stop balls that are thrown wild. He must be able to get off the first base bag quickly to prevent the ball from getting by him. He must also be good at scooping up a ball thrown in the dirt. Another common job is acting as the cut-off for balls thrown in from the outfield heading in the direction of home base.

A second baseman has to be capable of handling hard-hit balls and making the throw to the preferred base. This player also needs a baseball sense knowing when to cover second base and when and where to be as the cut-off for balls coming in from the outfield. Age and arm strength is not as important since whichever base he is throwing to is not very far.

The shortstop is considered to be the leader of the defense once a ball is put into play. Shortstops must have a strong throwing arm along with knowledge which comes mostly from experience, so they can direct their teammates on each play. The shortstop is also usually a twelve-year-old, but I have even had ten year olds capable of handling the job.

Third basemen play the position which is referred to as the "hot corner". Many balls are hit very hard at them, therefore, requiring them to be a good fielder. They are also responsible for handling balls that have been bunted in their surrounding area. They also must have a strong throwing arm in order to make a long, accurate throw to first base.

Last, but not least, are the outfielders on the team. Center-fielders pretty much run the outfield, like the shortstop runs the infield. They are usually fast runners who can cover a lot of ground. They are responsible for backing up the left fielder and right fielder and are often found chasing down the ball should it get by the other two fielders. Their age is not as much of a factor as their speed, their capability of catching fly balls, and a strong arm.

The left fielder and right fielder should be capable of catching fly balls and stopping balls that drop in front of them or towards their side. It's nice if they have a strong throwing arm, but since they usually throw the ball into the cut-off, strength is not a factor. They also are responsible for backing up the infielders. It is usually a nine-year-old that plays in the outfield, not because of their age, but because there are a lot fewer responsibilities they need to learn. Most nine-year-olds are not experienced enough and ready to play in the infield.

The remaining players on the team also have a job to do during a game. They should be standing up along the fence of the dugout, cheering on their team-mates on the ball field and offering them encouragement throughout the game. I constantly remind the players in the dugout to watch the game closely so they can learn the job of the players on the ball field, so when it's their turn to play a position they will know what to do. Much of their learning of the game comes from observation whether they are nine-, ten- or eleven-year-olds or a first year twelve-year-old.

Quite often a parent of a nine- or ten-year-old asks me if his child is ever going to play in the infield during a game. I try to explain to them that experience is necessary first. In practices they are given the opportunity to play infield, which gives them a little hands on experience. I also explain that it would be embarrassing to everyone, especially their child, if they were assigned to an infield position and were not quite sure of their responsibilities. Most of all, I don't want to take a chance of them getting hurt. What upsets some of the parents is when I play a nine- or ten-year-old in an infield position. This is the child that has baseball knowledge and who usually comes from a baseball-oriented family. The child has an advantage and can step right in and play as well as some twelve-year-olds. I try explaining that to the parents and tell them that it may take time, but eventually their child will be playing an infield position. It takes time for a nine-year-old to develop as a ball player, just like it takes time for them to be comfortable and accepted on the team. Nine-year-olds in their first year on a major league team usually doesn't say a word all year because they are so nervous. They come out of their shell as they enter into their second year as a ten-year-old, acting like a totally different person with no fears at all.

I strongly recommend to the parents of the nine- and ten-year-olds that they suggest to their children that they try to play on an All-Star team during the summer, which would give their child the opportunity to better themselves as players. It would be totally different from the regular season since they would be playing with and against teams their same age. That in itself is a morale booster for the child when they find out they can play much better against children their own age.

For years, youth baseball at the Major League level was played only by boys. Gradually, girls joined in the mix. Over the years, I coached numerous girls at the Minor League and Major League levels, as well as one girl on one of the All Star teams I managed. I found that girls were good listeners, worked hard at practices, were quick learners, well-behaved, and never complained or talked back to my coaches or me. Some of the boys, on the other hand, were just the opposite. When the girls showed up for practice, that is what they did. The boys quite often wanted to horse around instead of practice, if they could. Most girls could compete with boys through age twelve, but after that, boys usually had an edge on them.

There were many boys that took practice seriously, like the girls, and there were others that loved to be dramatic when diving for balls and then rolling on the ground. At times they overdid, hoping to be noticed by their coaches with hopes of being recognized as a great player. I always told the players to give a little extra and get their pants dirty, but what they did was a case of "Acting 101". There was one thing known as good hustle and another known as putting on a show. Many times the player couldn't get up off the ground quickly enough to finish the play which could have been completed if the player fielded the ball normally. Had the player finished off the dramatic play, the extra effort might have been appreciated more.

Even though I covered the topic of playing time at my team/parent meeting prior to the start of the season, questions continually came up once the regular season began. As much as I felt as though I were being fair, it was usually the parents and not the players that needed to understand my situation.

I started off explaining to them that in youth baseball games, there were only six innings, unlike professional major league baseball games which were nine innings. Every child would love to play all six innings, I understood, but unfortunately, it was impossible. Normally the twelve-year-olds were those that played a full six innings, with the remaining slots in the line-up being split amongst the other players. Depending upon the number of twelve-year-olds on the team, it wasn't always possible for all of them to play a full six innings. It was even occasionally, a ten- or eleven-year-old who could be one of the six inning players if their performance was above par.

In a game in which the visiting team was losing after five and one half innings, there was no need to play a sixth inning of defense. That meant it would limit playing time even more in some games. In certain situations, even in a six- inning game, some players only get two at bats which meant that the substitute players could just barely get their one at bat. Unless the players and parents understood how difficult it was for the manager to fulfill a substitute's required playing time, they just assumed that the manager wasn't being fair.

Twelve-year-old players and their parents automatically thought that all twelve-year-olds should be six inning players, yet that is not necessarily how it worked. The harder a player worked at practice and the more he developed as a player was what determined the individual's playing time, whatever the age. Unfortunately, it was very difficult to keep everyone happy.

Only once did a player himself ask to speak with me after a game about playing time. It was a twelve-year-old boy who I commended for being mature. His question was why, he, being a twelve-year-old, did not play six innings in every game. I first asked him who he thought were the

Dr. Alden

unquestionable six-inning ball players on the team. He named four twelve-year-olds and even one eleven-year-old. With that answer, I explained to him that would leave four slots in the lineup for me to fill with the remaining eight players on the team, him being one of them. I further explained that in each of the four slots, there would be two players who would have to share playing time. He then understood why six twelve-year-olds could not always play six innings in every game. I wished parents could only understand as easily as he did.

A Glutton For Punishment

12

Put Me In Coach

    Each week there were at least two games, one weeknight game and one game on Saturday. There were also two or three weeks where there was an additional weeknight game scheduled.

    Prior to the start of a weekday game, I always had my team arrive one hour early for a session of soft toss. At one of the complexes, a section of fence had been erected for that purpose. At the other ball fields, soft toss was hit directly into the backstop. Someday, all of the ball fields should have sections of fence erected for soft toss since the continuous batting of baseballs into the backstops causes the fencing to become distorted and become detached from the fence posts, resulting in the need for constant repairs. Either one of my coaches or I, give each player one or two buckets of baseballs to hit. Once a bucket is emptied, the players are asked to pick up the balls, placing them in their batting helmet and then dumping them back into the bucket. Even after repeatedly telling them not to pick up one ball at a time and try tossing them into the bucket from five or six feet away, they would constantly ignore my request. The reason was because half of the time they would have to pick the balls up a second time because they missed the bucket. For some reason, they could not get it into their heads they were wasting valuable time in the process.

    Unfortunately, there wasn't enough time to have regular batting practice prior to a weekday game, but on Saturdays the team met at the nearby high school baseball field two hours prior to the start of the game. After a quick session of soft toss, each player received a good five minutes of batting practice which was thrown by one of our coaches. If we had a 9:00 A.M. game, we only had a session of soft toss at the ball field where the game was to be played. Waking a player up to be at the ball field for 8:00 A.M. was difficult enough for the parents, never mind the thought of having to get the child to the ball field for a 7:00 A.M. batting practice. It took the players at least an hour to wake up once they got to the ball field at 8:00 A.M., so after they had their session of soft toss, I had the kids run a lap around the baseball complex just to make sure they were fully awake. A 9:00 A.M. game wasn't only dreaded by the players, but also by the coaches since we knew how much work it took to prepare each child just to play a baseball game.

Prior to the start of a game, after the team had loosened up and done their stretching exercises, I brought them into the dugout for the pre-game talk. First, I reminded the players of their responsibilities at each of their positions. If they had made mistakes in the previous game, we would have tried correcting them during practice, and then it was time to refresh their memory on what they had to do differently in the upcoming game. Many times I would have to address the same mistakes they were making game after game. Once the team took the field, I only hoped they remembered everything we had discussed. I often had to remind my coaches, and myself, that they were only nine-, ten-, eleven-, and twelve-year-olds since at times we all had a tendency to forget we were not dealing with adults.

Next, each team was given the opportunity to take the field for ten minutes of fielding practice. I found that when the kids were very sloppy and made numerous mistakes, we more often than not would have a good game. If they were flawless, I didn't have a very good feeling, since they usually played just the opposite. It's funny how it worked, but the outcome of the game usually followed that pattern. If it was a Saturday after the team had a two hour batting practice, quite often I would skip our turn for fielding practice, since the kids were already pretty well warmed up from tracking down balls, although, it could have been me just not wanting a preview of the game.

One of my most memorable days was when prior to the start of one of our games, the assistant coach of the opposing team was talking to me about how our season was progressing. We had been struggling all year long and our record was 3-14. He asked if I minded if he spoke with my team before the game, since he could tell the kids were all depressed. I told him that I didn't mind, since I thought he was a very nice individual who cared a lot about children. He just wanted to encourage my team not to give up, but to keep working hard and, most importantly, have fun. It was the same speech I had given my team many times before, and hearing it from someone else I hoped would give the kids a good boost. The coach wished them good luck and headed back to his dugout. The talk he gave must have really motivated my team because they went on to win the game 15-1. After the game, their coach asked me not to tell the manager of his team about his pre-game pep talk. There were still four games left in the regular season, and their team was still fighting to get into the playoffs. The coach must have thought they were going to beat us which would have qualified them for the playoffs that day. They ended up losing their next two games before winning their next to the last game of the season which finally qualified them for the playoffs. I can't see their coach giving another one of his motivational speeches again right away, since I could only assume he was sweating it out the last few games.

Before a game begins, what most parents don't understand is that a manager has to have a game plan. The most difficult planning involves who will be the next pitcher, if needed, and who will be the back-up catcher, if needed. A manager can't take anyone off the bench whenever he wants to, since there are rules regarding substitutions which have to be followed. Advance planning to a certain extent has to be in place. The job of working thirteen players into a game is more difficult than one may think. Even with a game plan, situations may change due to unexpected circumstances. One of the biggest factors is how well or how poorly a player is doing at bat and whether or not they should be substituted. If a player hits a home run and I had originally planned on removing him from the line-up for a substitute, it would be quite difficult to follow through with that choice. Situations like that occur during a game which make it so difficult for parents to understand how difficult it is for the manager, since parents usually just focuses on their child.

If a player does not attend soft toss or soft toss/batting practice prior to the game, for whatever reason, he is told that if he is not present thirty minutes prior to the start of the game, I will change my pre-determined lineup. I can't wait any longer than that, since there are things I have to do within those last thirty minutes to prepare the team for the game. I always ask the parents to let me know ahead of time if their child will be running late, unless it's an unexpected situation. A manager has to have sufficient time for his pre-game routine, and unless there are unforeseen circumstances, the players should be on time.

There were two instances which upset me immensely, and they were both about soccer games which players on my team had played in just prior to our baseball game. Neither of the children's parents informed me ahead of time that their child had a soccer game, for fear I would be upset. The one situation that bothered me most was when prior to our 9:30 A.M. Saturday game, I was reading the line-up for the game to the team. The child that I had announced who would be pitching told me that he wouldn't be able to pitch because he was very tired since he had just played in a soccer game at 7:30 A.M. He had arrived later than I had asked the team to arrive for soft toss prior to the game, and he looked like he was a little more tired than most of the other players looked considering it was a Saturday morning. Had I known that he had an early soccer game prior to our baseball game, I would have scheduled someone else to pitch. His parents didn't have the common courtesy to let me know a day ahead and didn't realize the inconvenience it causes me, the manager, when I have to rearrange the whole line-up due to their ignorance. I had previously asked parents with players on my team who also played soccer to either give me a schedule of their child's soccer games or at least let me know a few days in advance of back to back games.

The other situation involved a soccer player who was running late for our game. I received a call on my cell phone from his mother stating that he would be a little bit late for the baseball game. A little bit late, ended up being three innings late which was half of the game. When the child finally arrived, he was upset I didn't put him in the game immediately, and when I put him in the game I didn't put him in his regular position of shortstop. There was no reason I couldn't have been told ahead of time that the child was going to be late, but unfortunately some parents just can't understand how much aggravation it causes, not only for the manager, but for the team as a whole.

Once game time arrived and we were to take out our bats, I assumed the position of the third base coach. From there, I gave our batters and base runners a visual sign using my hands. The signs I used were not complicated like some of the signs that some managers used. There were signs to hit away, bunt, take a pitcher, steal a base, or to try a delayed steal. Prior to each pitch, the players were supposed to step out of the batter's box and look at me for a sign and then step back into the batter's box to bat.

Dr. Alden

The nine-year-olds, when taking their turn at bat, were often so nervous that they forgot to look at me for the sign, yet occasionally it was even a twelve-year-old that either forgot to look at me for a sign or just felt like doing what he wanted to do.

I constantly reminded each player that it was not necessary to hit a home run every time at bat, that a base hit was sufficient. Just making contact with the ball was a good start to generate runs which was the object of the game. A nine-year-old on my team couldn't understand why his previous coach told him to try and hit the ball square when he was using a round bat trying to hit a round ball. Once I explained to him hitting a ball square meant making contact with the bat directly on the center of the ball, he understood. When a player hit any part of the ball, I told him and everyone else, I was happy. Every ball player wanted to hit at least one home run in his youth baseball career, but not every player did. There was one year a ten-year-old on my team hit his first home run, then never hit another one after that. Every time he batted after getting the home run, he tried to hit another home run which prevented him from becoming a good hitter. If he just focused on getting a base hit, he probably would have been a better than average batter.

Whenever I gave the batter a bunt sign, if the circumstances warranted so, the parents of the batter usually were upset. Parents hate to see their child bunt, preferring to see them swing the bat with hopes of getting a solid hit. Sometimes a bunt is as good as a hit, which they don't understand. Whether a batter bunts the ball or hits the ball solidly, my coaches and I constantly tell them not to look at the ball, but run as fast as they can. When a player bunts a ball they never seem to slow down while running to first base, but when a player hits a ball solidly they have a tendency to watch the ball before running or either slow down or give up and stop running altogether, if they think the fielder is going to get them out. When a player is running to any base other than first base, I always tell them once they are approaching the furthest base possible of reaching, they should get their pants dirty, meaning to slide into the base. There was a much better chance of them being safe if they slide into the bases versus arriving at the base standing up. No matter how many times I tried reinforcing the need to slide, many of the players still would not slide. The players that did slide into the bases made me happy, especially the player one year who went through two pairs of uniform pants and almost a third, not only because he got his pants very dirty, but because of the holes he tore in his pants from sliding so much. Many times if a runner ran as fast as he could, as soon as he hit the ball, he would have been safe, since it is common for a fielder to either bobble the ball or make a bad throw to the base. It doesn't matter how many times you tell the runner, he just doesn't listen. What's even worse, on the other end of the spectrum, is when a coach tells a runner to stop at a base yet they continue running to the next base and get thrown out.

Once a runner gets on base, a manager occasionally replaces them with a courtesy runner under certain circumstances. A young nine- or ten-year-old player without much experience running the bases is often replaced. Even an eleven- or twelve-year-old is replaced, depending on the situation. A player can only be replaced once a game, but when the game is close, it pays to have an experienced or faster-running player on the bases. Parents sometimes wonder why their child who seldom gets on base is replaced once he finally gets on base, until I explain to them why. The player and parents usually understand, but they both still seem a little unhappy. It can make a big difference, especially in a close game.

There are occasional distractions that a manager has to deal with once a game has begun. One distraction that bothered me most was when a player came up to me in the middle of a game and asked if he could pitch, catch, play first base or so on and so forth. I always told the players on my team to talk to me at practice about a position they wanted to play, and I would take it into consideration, since there was too much going on during a game to be interrupted with a question like that. A player once told me, during the game, he would like to play catcher, and he was wearing his protective cup. He was only ten years old and his first year on the team. He struggled to catch a ball in an upright position, never mind the catcher's position. I told him I would let him try playing the catcher's position in practice first before playing the position in a game. This was the same player that stood on his "tippy toes" when I told the team they had to be on their toes at all times, so if a ball was hit to them they would be ready to field it. I honestly don't think he did it to be wise, he just he didn't get the gist of it.

Players also have to be consoled when struggling offensively and defensively. They get frustrated and tell everyone they can't play baseball and they want to quit. My coaches and I tell them that everyone has a bad game or two and will eventually get through their tough times. Many players are upset with themselves during a game and will call a time out and ask to speak with me. They use the imaginary injury or illness excuse such as having wicked headaches, upset stomachs, twisted ankles, or sore thumbs to name a few, as the reason to why they were not playing well. I tell them that all players from tee ball to professionals go through periods of frustration but eventually will pull through. I try to explain that a professional baseball player that gets one hit out of three tries is considered a pretty decent hitter. Most tears are shed when a player strikes out or is called out on strikes, yet not as many tears are shed when they hit the ball and make an out. One of the biggest reasons players have trouble hitting the ball is because the bat they are using is too big for them. Many players use a bat that is a couple of inches longer than they should be using along with being much too heavy for them. They think the bigger the bat, the farther they will hit the ball. Unfortunately, they and their parents who purchase the bat don't understand that it's harder to get the bat around quickly since it's so heavy, yet with a shorter and lighter bat it would be much easier to swing the bat.

One year I had a twelve-year-old on my team who was so unhappy with his batting that he just wanted to lay on the bench in the dugout and watch the game. He claimed that he wasn't feeling well, so I suggested that he tell his parents who were watching the game. He refused to tell them, but he agreed to sit up on the bench. Before I could tell his parents that he wasn't feeling well, his mother came over to me in the dugout and started hollering at me because her son wasn't playing. Even after I explained to her what was going on, she was still very upset with me and said that he wasn't sick, but unhappy because he hasn't started the game. Before the third inning began, he rushed outside the dugout and vomited before his parents decided to take him home.

As often as players threaten to quit, the majority of them stick it out and eventually pull through. At times even managers and coaches in the league get to the point where they consider quitting, but survive. If a coach on my team threatens to quit, I just tell them they can't leave or their child will go with them. That changes their mind quickly, even though they know I'm kidding.

In any sport, defense wins games. In baseball, you still have to score a few runs, but with good defense you can limit the number of runs scored by the opponent. In a well pitched game, as I mentioned previously, the defensive players have very little to do in the field. It's nice to breeze along, but at times it can become quite boring. The manager and coaches have to keep the fielders alert and ready to make a play at all times. The outfielders tend to become bored much more quickly than the infielders. It is usually the nine- or ten-year-old who is in the outfield that I compare to cows that have been put out to pasture to graze. Usually with little to do, they have a tendency to look around the area, quite often spotting friends watching the game, who in turn distract the players. While not being focused on the game when a ball is hit to them, there's a good chance they won't make the play. Staying focused is very important for every player in the field, and the best way to keep focused is to keep an eye on the batter at all times so they will be ready to make the play.

It's not only their friends that distract them, but it's also their parents. When the parents are sitting in the bleachers or standing along the sidelines, cheering for the team is acceptable, but when a parent decides to stand directly behind the backstop behind home base when the child is pitching, that is not acceptable. A child pitching is under enough pressure without having the mother or father staring at him which causes even a bigger distraction. I hate having to ask the parents to move to another location, since they feel as though they are helping their child as they offer them encouragement.

Parents in the bleachers or along the sidelines at times also like to offer instruction to their children, which oftentimes is not the same instruction being given by the manager or coaches. In one particular game, which was very close, a player's father gave his son the sign to steal second base. The boy was thrown out, and when I asked the child if the first base coach sent him, he said it was his father's idea. Cheering for a child is fine as long as they keep it generic. Parents being too supportive such as offering their own instructions can sometimes do more harm than good.

Once a game has ended, I gather the team together inside the dugout or outside of the dugout if there is another game to follow. Whenever a team loses a close game, they always remember the mistake or mistakes that were made closest to the end of the game. A good example is when a player commits an error which results in the winning run being scored. That play is fresh in his mind as well as in the minds of the rest of the team and the player and his teammates automatically attribute the loss of the game to that one play. When you look back over the course of the game at other mistakes, errors, or lack of hitting by the team, then they realize that there was more than just that one play which decided the game. Many players blame themselves and take it personally. I know I have blamed myself on numerous occasions for losing a game because I made the wrong decision. Many times, I went home after a game and laid in bed thinking about the game and what I should have done differently. I know exactly how that child must have felt when he went to bed after blaming himself for the loss. I tried not to focus only on what we had done wrong during a game and what we could do differently the next game, but I also talked about the positive things the team did during the game.

If we won the game, I quickly reviewed the highlights and presented the game ball to the individual who had an outstanding game. If a player had hit a home run in the game, the parent would chase down the ball and hold onto it as a keepsake.

The most memorable post game talk I gave was commending one of my teams that turned a triple play in a game. The umpire had called the infield fly rule, which ruled the batter out. There were runners on all three bases, all of whom took off running instead of staying on their respective base as they should have done. Our pitcher, who had caught the fly ball, threw to the third baseman covering third base who in turn threw to the second baseman covering second base to complete the triple play since the base runners didn't get back to their bases in time. Our second baseman even had enough time that he could have thrown to the first baseman covering first base for another out which obviously was not necessary.

Once I had finished speaking with the team, I always asked my coaches if they had anything they would like to add. After they were given the opportunity, I gave the players a chance to say a few words if they wished to. It was then time to pick up all of the equipment and bring it to my truck unless there were any other comments.

If it was one of the player's birthdays, the parents usually brought along a couple of dozen cupcakes for the team and the coaches, which sent everyone home with loads of energy due to a sugar high. Once in a while after a game, a parent or I, would treat the team to a fruit-flavored frozen slush from the concession stand. The most popular choice was what they called the suicide slush. It consisted of a small squirt of each flavor, which to me was the weirdest-tasting concoction you could imagine. It didn't matter if it was 35 degrees or 85 degrees outside, they still lined up for them. On special occasions, a parent, coach or I treated the team to an ice cream at the nearby soft-serve ice cream stand. That, without saying, was the best treat of all.

P.S. I heard there was one team in the league with a player who had never made contact with the ball, other than fouling back a ball, until towards the end of his fourth year on the team. He either struck out swinging or was called out on strikes whenever he got up to bat. Then one day the manager of the team presented him with the game ball when he finally drilled a foul ball down the right field line, which was the closest he ever came to getting a hit. It sounded a bit silly giving him the ball for that, but I understood the player was very happy and wore a big smile on his face for a week.

13

LINE DRIVES

Why is the expression, "Heads Up" used when a foul ball is hit into a crowd of spectators? If a spectator lifts his head up, there is more of a chance of being hit in the face. If the expression "Heads Down" were used, the person could lean his head down while covering the head and face, which would minimize the seriousness of an injury. Almost every baseball field in youth baseball has an adjacent field with the area in between the two fields being a target for foul balls. It's a wonder that spectators rarely get beaned or severely injured from a stray ball. Most people think that a batter or fielder in a game is the only person in danger of getting hit by a baseball, but spectators have almost as much chance of being hit, considering how many foul balls are hit in just one game. For some reason, spectators are seldom hit.

If I had extra money that I could invest in stocks, I would choose to buy stock from the company that manufactures icepacks. The number of cases used during baseball season across the world must be phenomenal. A player either warming up before a practice or a game or when playing a position in the field who gets hit by a baseball is probably the person on the team that uses the most icepacks. Next, would be the batter that got hit by a pitched baseball. Finally, it would be the base runner who gets hit by a bad throw. In each of these cases, a coach almost immediately pulls out an icepack and offers it to the child to ease the pain.

A coach is the adult next most frequently hit by a baseball. When hitting baseballs to the fielders during practice, a coach must watch for poorly thrown baseballs being thrown to the person catching for them. I have been pretty lucky as far as not getting hit in the head, but I have been hit in the back on numerous occasions. It reminds me of what type of pain children go through when they are hit by a baseball themselves. Whenever a player gets hit by a baseball, one of my coaches always tells the child, "It only stings for a few minutes." That may be true, but what he doesn't tell them is starting later that day, it will ache for about a week.

It's hard to believe, but a coach pitching batting practice is rarely hit by a baseball. Pitching to a batter only forty-six feet away is a dangerous task, yet most coaches have good reflexes. A protective pitching screen is used by some coaches to prevent being hit by a batted baseball yet most coaches don't want the inconvenience of having to drag it out of the storage trailer and then have to put it back at the end of practice.

Before our league purchased the protective pitching screen, I had a couple of close calls myself. One batter I was pitching to, a very strong twelve-year-old with a powerful swing of the bat, hit a line drive back to me which I caught but literally knocked me over backwards. That woke me up real quick. The second close call I had came as I was pitching to a different twelve-year-old batter. He also hit a line drive back to me, which I frantically reached down to catch as it was about to hit me directly in my "family jewels". I successfully caught the ball, yet I had to take a couple of minutes to compose myself. The next day I went out and purchased a protective cup, which I wore faithfully, thereafter.

I continued to pitch batting practice for a few more years, until I drafted a nine-year-old player whose father offered to help coach. He enjoyed coaching, yet he loved to pitch batting practice to the players more than anything else. A few years later, I selected his second son to play on the team also. After six years of coaching with his children, I asked if he would be interested in staying on as a coach once his two sons had moved on to the next level of play. He said he'd love to stay and that he would help me out in any area where I needed him. I said he could continue pitching batting practice since he was a "rubber arm coach", who could pitch forever without getting tired. I will refer to him as Rac, hereafter.

Rac was very good with the kids yet was stricter with them than I was. He always pushed the kids to do better and better at every practice. Many of the players over the years asked him if he was ever happy, because the kids thought he only wanted perfection from them. He said that he was happy when everyone tried to do their best as long as they tried to remember to do what he worked so hard to teach them.

Rac could pitch batting practice for a longer period of time than any other coach I have ever seen. He could pitch indefinitely, and his reflexes were like those of a tiger. He could snag line drives out of mid-air. He always refused the offer of using the protective pitching screen, even when I told him I would bring it out for him.

One day he took a direct hit to the face from a baseball hit so fast that he didn't have time to react. He hit the ground with blood pouring from his face, but he said he was all right and could continue pitching. After I suggested, along with another one of my coaches, that he should go to the hospital for stitches, he agreed after looking at his face in a mirror. The following day he arrived to practice, with glove in hand and ready to pitch batting practice again. A few years later, he took another direct hit to the face that knocked him to the ground which dazed him for a few minutes. He was bleeding pretty heavily again this time, yet said he was O.K. and would continue pitching batting practice. All of my coaches and all of the parents in attendance and I said, "No way." He said he would drive himself to the hospital after he refused offers from a few people.

I resumed practice with another one of my coaches taking on the duty of pitching. Even after Rac had been hit in the face for the second time, the coach taking over for him refused my offer of bringing out the pitch screen. The first pitch to the same batter that sent Coach Rac to the hospital hit another line drive like a bullet which hit a teammate's mother in the face. She was standing outside of the playing area behind the fence beside the bleachers. The ball just cleared the fence and hit her like a lead balloon. She had a cut which did not require any stitches, but it really shook her up and made her pretty sore for about a week. Once we got her composed, we were ready to resume play. The batter was pretty shook up, himself, and he told me to let the next batter take his turn. He said he had done enough damage for one day. After Rac had gone to the hospital for stitches, I said to the other coaches, I wished I had told him what he always told a player when they got hit by a batted ball, "It only stings for a minute." I'm sure he would have got a big kick out of that. Over the years, I've seen numerous coaches get hit by foul balls in the arm or leg during a game. Some coaches stand outside the fenced in dugout like they are lined up in front of a firing squad. I always stay behind the fence, since I don't feel like taking a chance of getting hit by a line drive.

One day, during a game, the manager of the team we were playing took a line drive to his head. He was standing outside the fenced -in dugout, and he could hardly stand up after being hit. It was the most frightening situation I saw prior to the day Rac got hit in the face the second time. It's dangerous enough to be coaching at third base sixty feet away from the batter during a game, never mind twenty-five or thirty feet away in front of the dugout. For many years, only one adult coach was allowed to coach a base, with the second coach being a player. It seemed so idiotic to let a nine-year-old coach a base even when wearing a batting helmet, especially when a good-sized twelve -year-old got up to bat. I always moved back another ten feet myself because I knew how fast a ball could be hit off the bat by a twelve year old. Eventually, the league changed the rules to allow two adult coaches to coach the bases, one at first base and one at third base. I have never been hit by a foul ball while coaching third base, knock on wood, but I've had some close encounters. Most managers use two adults to coach the bases, yet occasionally they will use one adult coach and one player as the second coach. Within the past few years, professional Major League Baseball required the first base coach and the third base coach to wear protective helmets. It wouldn't be a bad idea if our league followed suit.

What seems even more bizarre is when the manager or coach of a team brings his infielders in to the edge of the infield grass when one of the tallest and strongest twelve-year-olds gets up to bat. I feel like telling the fielders, as I stand coaching third base, to back up to where they were and not listen to their coach. It's a wonder that there are not more injuries to the children playing infield due to hard hit line drives hit directly at them. The pitcher is the closest person to the batter at only forty-six feet away, and whether it be a short nine-year-old, a tall twelve-year-old or a forty-year-old coach, there is always a chance of getting hit by a line drive and being seriously hurt.

A collision between two fielders can be as dangerous as being hit by a line drive. When two fielders are attempting to catch a ball, one of them should tell the other one that he will try to make the catch. Once a player calls out that it's his ball to catch, the second, or even a third fielder, should back off. The coaches stress over and over, in practice, for players to "call for it", to prevent the players from colliding. There is nothing worse than seeing two or more fielders lying on the ground motionless after colliding with each other, not knowing how seriously they may be injured and whether or not they will need medical attention.

14

Playoffs

    The goal of any child on any team in any sport is to make it to the playoffs and then win the championship. The same is true for the manager and the coaches. After all, isn't that the reason for playing any sport? As much as a game should be played for the purpose of having fun, you have to agree that everyone wants to win. It's nice to be the Division Champions, but winning it all is the dream of every child. It takes talented players, hard work, and even a little bit of luck. If parents get upset with the coach's philosophy of winning, maybe they should take the kids to a ball field, let them make up the teams, and let the kids play without coaching. Maybe the kids would have a lot more fun.

    It was only my second year as a Major League manager, and my team made it to the playoffs. We had a group of talented players, a team that practiced very hard, and some good luck. It came down to the last game of the season and we had to win to get into the playoffs. It was the last game of the day, and it would conclude the regular season. If we won, we would beat out the team that was tied with us, and if we lost they would go to the playoffs because they had beaten us two out of three times during the regular season. The manager of the team we were to play had promised one of his twelve-year-olds that he could pitch since he had never pitched before, and it was the last game he would be playing in the league because he would be moving up to the next level the following year. Winning the game was not important, since the team had no chance of making the playoffs, unlike the team that was tied with us. The manager stuck to his word and pitched his twelve-year-old first-time pitcher. We won the game and made it into the playoffs through the so-called "backdoor," better known as luck, in this case. Sometimes a team that has already clinched a spot in the playoffs will also not use one of their better pitchers for the final few games of the regular season, so they can rest them for the playoffs. What happens occasionally, is when there are two teams fighting to get the final spot in the playoffs, one of the teams faces a weaker pitcher of the team already in the playoffs and beats them, while the other team they were in contention with faces a team with a stronger pitcher not headed to the playoffs and ends up losing. A situation like that can be frustrating.

The first round of the playoffs was a best of three game series. Like most playoff games, Game One was a very close, exciting game. We had made it to the last inning and were leading 2-1 but had run out of our regularly used pitchers. The only pitcher that had any experience in pitching was one of our nine-year-old players. He was tall for his age and threw left-handed. I had no choice but to put him into the game to pitch. His father happened to be one of my coaches, and I told him we had to give it a shot as much as I hated to put the pressure on a nine-year-old. I heard the child's mother who was sitting in the bleaches next to the dugout say, "Why is the coach putting a nine-year-old in to pitch?" Like most parents, she was not aware that I had run out of pitchers, and I had no other choice than to use her son.

My nine-year-old came into the game and retired the first two batters. He then walked the next batter, bringing up a good-size twelve-year-old who was one of the best hitters on the team. After the first two pitches, which were balls, the nine-year-old threw a pitch right down the middle of the plate. We still had a one run lead and needed only one more out. The batter hit a hard line drive deep to right field but directly to our twelve-year-old right fielder who caught the ball. The game was over. We won. The nine year old rookie's mom and dad were very proud of him and couldn't believe he had saved the game. Thanks to him, he made me look good, even though I didn't have any other choice. The manager of the team we had just beaten was none other than my friend Pie. We won Game Two by a score of 18-11, became the Division Champions and were headed to the championship series.

The players and coaches on our team knew we would be facing a very good team from the other division in the next series. They had a history of winning many championships over the years. We, the coaches, tried very hard to build confidence in our team, since they didn't feel as though they had a chance of winning any games. Our team practiced very hard and was determined to play the best they could and come off with a win. One of the players on our team made some positive comments that he hoped would motivate his teammates. He also said our team worked very hard to get to this point and that whether we won or lost the series we would still be getting "hardware" - hardware meaning a trophy even if we were the runners-up. To make a long story short, we ended up being beaten two games straight. The pitching on the other team was the difference in the games. As everyone knows, pitching is a very important part of the game of baseball.

A few years passed before our next appearance in the playoffs, but this time we made it through the front door without assistance. Our team was much stronger than the previous team that had made it to the playoffs. In Game One, we faced the top pitcher in the league and got beat up pretty good, as I expected we would. I had used one of my weaker pitchers knowing that we didn't have a pitcher that could compare to their Ace. I basically gave them the first game of the three game series and depended on my two top pitchers to win the next two games. The other team only had to win one of their next two games, which made them the favorites. Their team was already planning their party, and their kids were all smiles. We knew we would have to take it one game at a time, and it would still be very hard to beat them. We won the second game of the series, much to the surprise of the other team. This meant it would go to a third game, and there was no favorite. Both teams had played an exciting Game Two, and if any team had a better player pitching in Game Three, it would be us. Game Three was played as expected, very intense, but we came away with the win. We were headed to the Championship Series.

The team we were to play next was also a strong team like ours. They had won the championship the previous year, and a good number of their players knew what playoffs were all about. We felt we could give them a good run, even though their pitching was a little stronger than ours. Their pitching turned out to be a lot stronger than expected, and we ended up losing two games in a row. The kids took it pretty hard, but within a few days you never would have known they had lost the championship. They still had played a good season of baseball even though they didn't win it all, and they were still happy that they would be getting "hardware." Kids have a tendency to bounce back quickly, but I took longer than they did.

A coach always tries to figure out what he did wrong and what he should have done differently. I finally got over it, but not until I reminded myself what I always told my teams, "It's only a game."

I'm waiting patiently for the next appearance in the playoffs, and I'm hoping the saying "Third time never fails" applies to my team. As I said before, everyone wants to win it all, but the most important thing everyone should remember is to have fun whether you win or lose. A team still can have fun even if they don't make it into the playoffs. Sometimes there's a chance to prevent another team from getting into the playoffs, even if you have had a terrible season. It's not quite as good as winning a championship, by any means, but at least if the kids play as hard as they can right to the end, it's better than giving up with three or four games left in the season, as I've seen some teams do.

15

All-Stars - A Summer Of Fun (Usually)

THE EXPECTED

Coaching an all-star team was a fun way to end the baseball season. The all-star teams were made up of players from the Major League division and were chosen by the Major League division managers. After each manager had nominated the players from his own team, they all had the opportunity to nominate any player from the other teams if they felt a player had been overlooked. There was one all-star team selected consisting of eleven-and twelve-year-olds who played in a tournament that led to the opportunity to compete not only for the state championship, but also for the next levels beyond. A second team was selected from only twelve-year-olds and was referred to as the 12-B team. There were two all-star teams selected from the eleven-year-olds that were referred to as the 11-A team and the 11-B team. The same was done with the ten-year-olds that were referred to as the 10-A team and the10-B team. The final all-star team consisted of nine-year-olds; there was only one team for this age group. Thirteen players were voted onto each team except for the team comprised of eleven-year-olds and twelve-year-olds, which only had twelve. The manager of that team had the option of adding one or more players of his choice to the team if he so wished.

Dr. Alden

The manager with the best record from the previous year's regular season had the first choice for the team he preferred. Once he had chosen a team or declined the opportunity to coach a team, the next manager in line would be given his choice with the process continuing until each team had a manager. Most managers, even if they had a better record, would let a manager with a lower record take the team his child had been selected to play on. Occasionally, a manager would take a team ahead of the manager whose child was on the team, which at times would cause hard feelings. Most every manager looked forward to the opportunity to manage his son's or daughter's all-star team, if at all possible. Since I did not have a child playing in the league any longer, it was not a concern of mine and I knew that there were usually a few teams that would need a manager once every manager had been given the opportunity. Most every manager had assistance coaching their all-star teams from parents of the players on the team. More often than not these parents were assistant coaches during the regular season with their child's team. Oftentimes a manager would bring along his coaching staff from his regular season team since they enjoyed working together. Rac has helped me coach my all-star teams a number of years after his two boys were no longer playing in the league. He was always willing to help out where ever needed, especially pitching batting practice.

Each team was scheduled to play in three or four tournaments over the course of the summer. Some of the tournaments ran only one weekend from Thursday through Sunday or Friday through Sunday, while other tournaments were scheduled to run for two weekends. Each weekend, the teams were usually playing in different towns, although occasionally as many as three of the teams could be found playing in the same town on the same weekend. Parents having two children playing on two different all-star teams would usually take turns watching each child play if they were playing in different towns. If they were lucky, the whole family traveled back and forth to the different towns to see both children play if their schedules allowed sufficient travel time. If parents had three children playing all-stars, they were wished the best of luck.

The first year I became a Major League manager, I had the opportunity to manage an all-star team. Since it was my first year, I was put at the bottom of the list to choose a team. I did not care what team I got, I just wanted to manage a team. When it came to my turn, there was only one team left so I took the team and set out to have some fun.

The team that I ended up with was the 12-B all star team. I received a list of the players' names and phone numbers on the team. I was also given a practice schedule and a list of the tournaments they would be participating in. The following day I called each player to inform them when their first practice would be held. It would be a couple of weeks before all thirteen players could practice together as a team since the playoffs for the regular season were just beginning. The managers of the four teams in the playoffs usually preferred that their players only attended their own practices until they had either been eliminated or had completed the playoffs. The managers coaching the all-star teams understood and usually already knew a lot about the players on their all-star teams. Usually, only six to eight players attended the all-star practice for the first week unless the regular season managers in the playoffs allowed their players to attend. After the first week of playoffs ended, a few more players attended the all-star practices once two of the teams had been eliminated. After the second week, once every player could make it to the all-star practice, I spoke with them all. The first thing I told them was that they would be representing our town when we participated in the tournament and I expected them to be on their best behavior at all times. That meant not only during a game but also before and after games.

I then spoke to the players and their parents about the tournaments we would be playing in and how the rules of each tournament varied. The rules were usually much different than the rules we played by during the regular season. This is when I covered the issue of playing time and tried to explain that it was much more difficult substituting players in all-star games than it was during the regular season. I had watched all-star games in previous years and spoken with other managers, so I was well aware of what to expect.

Playing time was more of an issue with all-stars than it was during the regular season. Since every player on the all-star team was an all-star, every parent felt that his child was as good as the next one. Even being all-stars, there were usually five players that were the core of the team. They were a bit above the others offensively and defensively. That left the other four slots in the batting order to be divided among the eight remaining players. Occasionally the five core players would sit out during a game, but for the most part they played more innings than their teammates. Unfortunately, a lot of parents could not understand that was the way it worked.

Most every tournament had what was called a slaughter rule. When a team had a lead of ten runs or more after four complete innings, or three and one half innings if the home team was ahead, the game was over. Talk about cutting into playing time. If after two innings we had a big lead and if I could tell we were playing a weak team, I made my substitutions to make sure everyone got to play at least two of the four innings, in case we won by the "slaughter rule". Nine out of ten times, the game ended after four innings as I expected it would.

Another rule very common in tournaments was the "designated hitter". If we were playing in a tournament that gave the option of using a designated hitter, I would ask if anyone would like to take a turn being the designated hitter. It would give them a chance to rest, since they would not have to play defense in the field and they would only have to bat. Most every player thought it was great, so I let them take turns each game being the designated hitter. After one game, the parents of the child who was the designated hitter, came up to me and asked why their son didn't play defense during the game. I explained what I had done, and when they found that it was their child's own choice, they understood. From that day on, I always explained to the parents about the designated hitter rule and how I addressed it so there would be no questions as to what I did.

Other than when a player chose to be the designated hitter in a game, our league required that every player on each of the all-star teams got at least one time at bat and played defensively a minimum of six consecutive outs, regardless of the playing time requirements set forth for each tournament. The only team that did not have to abide by our league's rule was the eleven-and twelve-year-old team when they were participating in the tournament that could lead to the state championship. Then, they only had to fulfill the playing time requirements set forth for that tournament.

Prior to tournament games, we usually had batting practice at our hometown field. The kids then packed up and traveled with their parents to the town where the tournament was being held. If we knew there were batting cages available at the complex where the tournament was being held sometimes we would do our practice there. If there was more than one game scheduled that day, we usually only had the one batting practice at home, then the kids would rest in between games, since it was usually very hot.

During my years of coaching all-stars, I've had my ups and downs. There were always issues involving playing time, which I expected to have, and I dealt with. I knew what was coming when a parent came to me after a game and asked if I had a minute where they could talk to me. I always told them I did and prepared myself to answer the usual questions. Most parents usually think about only their child and do not look at the whole picture, which I understand. I had the thirteen players that I had to coach, and I tried to please their parents, which varied in numbers depending on the family situation. Between parents and step-parents, I had my hands full. At times I got the feeling I was being thrown into a cage full of lions or tigers, yet I successfully escaped before being devoured. I understood that every child wants to play six innings of baseball in every game, but that is mathematically impossible. As during the regular season, it was usually the individuals that were not in attendance for the meeting I held where I discussed playing time who caused the problems or complained about the issues I addressed prior to the start of the tournaments.

What really surprised me was the year the complainer about playing time was the father of a player from the team I managed during the regular season. Of course he did not show up to the pre-season meeting I held before the regular season began or the meeting I held prior to the start of the tournaments. At least that proved to the other parents of players on the all-star team that I did not show any favoritism, especially to one of my "own" players.

The last phase of the game I had to deal with was the selection of players to receive the awards at the end of each game. Certificates, trophies or some other form of awards were normally presented to the top three stars of the game. The first and third place awards were usually given to players from the winning team with the second place award usually going to a player from the losing team. It was best when a representative from the tournament made the selections, which made it easier on me. That way I didn't get accused of showing favoritism to any of my players. When I had to select the player or players for the award, I was always honest with who I felt played a good game. Many times, the same players received the awards game after game since they really did deserve it. Whenever I had to make the choice, it was a no-win situation for me. After playing their last game in each tournament, every player would receive a participation certificate from the tournament director. At least they received the recognition of being an all-star that way.

There were times where I made up special certificates myself for players on my teams who were never chosen to receive a star-of-the-game award. I called it "the unsung hero award", which I gave to a player that had played many good games but had been passed over time and time again since someone else had a little better game. When they received the certificate you could tell that they were very happy, and it really boosted their morale.

Even with all the little problems, the players and their parents seemed to have a lot of fun. Over the years, the kids won many tournaments, were the runners-up quite a few times, and overall won a good percentage of their games. Most every summer, the teams played as many as fifteen to twenty games, close to the number of games the kids played during the league's regular season.

One of the most memorable moments was when a twelve-year-old all-star, in his final year of youth baseball, finally hit his first home run. Hitting a home run is a dream that every child has. To see their facial expression when they hit their first home run told it all. Another memorable moment was when an all star team turned a triple play. That happened not only once when I was coaching an all-star team, but three times in three different years, each by a 10-A team. In youth baseball, turning a double play at the 10-A level seldom occurs, never mind a triple play. I'm sure the kids of those teams will remember the day they turned a triple play for years to come.

Unfortunately, every year there were a few unlucky ball players that did not get the opportunity to play on an all-star team. There are only so many slots available and always a handful of unhappy children and parents. It's a shame that young children have to get a taste of what life is all about at such a young age, but the only thing you can tell them is to keep working hard and to try again the next year.

I've heard that some towns selected their all-star teams much differently from our league. Their managers picked the age group they wanted to coach and then selected the players of their choice for their team. The only person "taking the heat" from an unhappy parent, must have been that lone manager when they "by-passed" a child for the hand-picked team. At least in our league, it wasn't just one manager that had to "take the heat"; here it could be spread out among all of the managers when a child was not selected to play on a team. Most everyone felt that our selection process gave every player a fair chance of getting selected for a team.

Coaching an all-star team involved many hours of practice, many long days playing tournament games and much time traveling to and from the tournament each day. The all-star season takes up a good part of the summer for the players, their friends, family, the coaches and manager. In the end, everyone looks back and usually agrees it was worth it.

At the conclusion of the all-star season, the players receive a team picture along with a participation certificate from our league. I also give each all-star team I coach a pizza party at a local pizza shop where they reminisce about their summer of baseball.

In the thirteen years since I became a manager in the Major League division, I managed an all- star team or assisted with coaching an all-star team almost every year. I managed two all-star teams consisting of eleven- and twelve-year-olds, numerous 12-B all-star teams, numerous 10-A all-star teams, and one year was an assistant coach helping Pie with his 11-A all-star team. Some day when I get the opportunity, I'm looking forward to managing a nine-year-old all star team, as I have yet to manage one. I hear it is a lot of fun at that age.

Dr. Alden

THE UNEXPECTED

Coaching an all-star team was also a challenge when unexpected situations arose. One of my most memorable experiences occurred during one of my all-star team's first practices. The team arrived for practice and proceeded to loosen up their arms by playing catch. Once everyone was warmed up, they followed with a series of stretching exercises and ran a lap around the field. Once the players had completed their run, I asked them to have a seat in the dugout. As they started filing into the dugout, a fight broke out between two of the players. Immediately, one of my coaches standing very close pulled the two of them apart ending the fist-punching incident. After speaking to the two boys outside of the dugout, I told one of them to sit on one end of the bench and the other one on the other end of the bench. This kept eleven players in between them as they sat on the bench. After speaking with all of the players in the dugout, practice resumed with no further incidents.

After practice had ended and the player's parents arrived to pick up their children, I spoke with the mother of one of the boys involved with the incident. I found out that the boys had gotten into a fight in school earlier that week and that both had been suspended from school. That was the first I had heard about it and I was very upset that no one had given me any warning. When the second boy's mother arrived, I spoke with both boys and their mothers stating that it had best be the last incident between the two boys or they both would both be asked to leave the team. They all agreed that there would be no more altercations and I told them I would do my part by keeping them as far apart from each other as possible at all times. From the next practice until the end of the all-star team's season, I could not believe how well the summer went, considering the way the first practice had started. There was not one incident to speak of.

There was another incident involving a player that caused me a considerable amount of embarrassment. It happened when I was the assistant coach of the 11A all-star team my friend Pie was managing. I had agreed to help him out at practices and during the games I would be the first base coach. It all started when one of our players hit a home run. He ran around the bases and as he was heading to home base he stopped about ten feet from the plate, fell flat on his stomach and flopped like a fish out of water moving forward until he reached the plate. The manager and coaches of the opposing team came out of the dugout, which was only a few feet from the coach's box that I was standing in, and proceeded to ask me what we were teaching our team. Their manager was very upset with the unnecessary display by our player, yet I was twice as upset as he was. I told him that we did not teach our players to "showboat" and that I had no idea what caused our player to act like that. I promised that it would never happen again. Pie called a time out once the play had ended and we both spoke with our disrespectful player. I felt like crawling into a hole but I headed back to the first- base coach's box. Soon after, play resumed. Over the years, there were numerous situations where the players from various all-star teams acted up occasionally, but you can't expect kids to be perfect all the time.

    Parents also have a tendency to become a little bit excited. There was a player on one of my all- star teams who was a good little fielder but had been struggling with his batting. All summer long, he could not hit the ball if his life depended on it. He was the best bunter on the team, so I usually had him bunt with hopes of generating some action on the bases. Nine out of ten times he laid down a perfect bunt and got on base. To me, a bunt single was as good as a full swing single. Unfortunately his father did not feel that way. During one game as his son was about to step into the batters box to bat, his father who was sitting out beyond the center field fence hollered out loud enough for everyone to hear, "let him hit the ball". I knew exactly what his father meant, he wanted him to swing the bat and not bunt like he usually did. I ignored his father's plea and gave his son the bunt sign. With runners on first base and second base, again he laid down a perfect bunt. I'm not sure but I thought I saw steam pouring out of his father's eyes and ears, two hundred feet away. Our opponent's third baseman came in, fielded the ball perfectly and threw to the first baseman. The ball sailed over the first baseman's head sending the ball into the foul territory in right field. Our base runners from first and second base scored and our all-star bunter ended up on third base. Two runs had scored and there was dead silence in center field. End of story.

    The most embarrassing situation that ever happened was at a tournament where two of the players' fathers each caused a commotion. I felt I had done a good job over the years with my all-star teams following my rules regarding good behavior, but after this particular day, I realized that in the future I would have to include the player's parents when giving my speech on good behavior as well.

Dr. Alden

The first incident occurred prior to the start of one of our games as our team was warming up on the field. I looked over toward the concession stand, which was about one hundred feet away, when I heard hollering and screaming. One of my player's fathers was complaining about how lousy the concession stand was and how filthy the portable toilets were. He had harassed the tournament directors so much that they came over to me prior to the start of the game and told me to do something about this ignorant parent or he would be thrown off the property. The directors knew what team the father was affiliated with due to the bright orange tee shirt he was wearing. The dead giveaway was due to the fact that the fans from our town were wearing bright orange tee shirts with black lettering; the same colors as our all-star team's shirts. It is our town's trademark and they are found at all of our tournaments regardless of what team was playing. It makes it very easy to find the field our teams are playing on, yet it can also put you in the spotlight. After I spoke with the player's father, he settled down and contained himself for the rest of the day.

As if the first incident wasn't bad enough, within fifteen minutes of when the game finally started, another father of one of my players also had a problem keeping his mouth shut. He complained from the start of the game about a particular umpire and would not quit. Finally, the umpire came over to our dugout and told me I had better tell the parent to keep his mouth shut or he would be thrown off the property. I spoke to the father but evidently he could not understand English since he continued to make a big scene. The umpire told him to leave the property, where upon he moved his truck to the side of the road where he watched the game from a distance. When the game ended, I asked the team to go sit on a stone wall about one hundred feet away at the edge of the complex while I spoke with their parents. I took the parents aside and read them the riot act about the two incidents that day. I can't remember ever being as upset as I was that day. After I had spoken with the parents, I apologized to the tournament directors about the parent's behavior and promised that it would never happen again.

Over the years there was one other situation that made me very angry. I was quite upset when I found out that there were parents paying their children anywhere between thirty-five dollars to one hundred dollars or more every time they hit a home run. The reason I was upset was because as a coach we stress to the players that all they have to do is get base hits and not to try to kill the ball for a home run. It was obvious why they tried to hit a home run since they would be making money. I found out that some players were paid by their parents even when they hit a home run in practice or during a regular season game. With parents like that, it didn't help out the coaches when teaching the players to play as a team.

16

ALL-STARS - THE LONG, ACTION-PACKED SUMMER

This all-star team was the team consisting of eleven-and twelve-year-old players. The managers from the Major League division selected the twelve players, with one of them being an eleven-year-old. I could have added up to three more players on the team, but I chose to keep it at twelve. If additional players were chosen, they would have to have been nominated prior to the initial selection of players. Most every year there would be at least one eleven-year-old either voted onto the team or selected afterward by the manager of the team. Whenever an eleven-year-old made this all-star team there were always complaints filed by the parents of the twelve-year-olds that were not selected. If the manager of the team elected to stay with only twelve players, there would be at least one child that had usually played with that same group of players as a nine-, ten-, or eleven-year-old all-star that did not make the team. If an eleven-year-old or a different twelve-year-old player was selected as one of the twelve players, there would be not only one or two children "left off" the team but now two or three. The reason an eleven-year-old was selected over a twelve-year-old, was usually justifiable.

The first three years I managed a Major League team, I had the opportunity to coach an all-star team each summer. Each of the three years I coached the 12 B All-Star Team. This year after the eleven- and twelve-year-old all star team had been selected, as every year, the managers from the Major League division got to choose if they were interested in coaching the team. This particular year, every manager was given the opportunity to take the team, yet no one was interested. My feeling was that none of the managers felt the team would do very well, so they all passed up the opportunity.

As in previous years, I had told the managers since I didn't have a child playing in the league, they could choose ahead of me if they were interested. When no one showed interest in taking the eleven-and twelve-year-old all star team I said that I would be excited to manage the team. I had not discussed with my wife the possibility of coaching an all-star team since I had planned on taking the summer off. I figured there wouldn't be any teams left to take after the other managers had taken their choice of teams. It was only that evening I decided to take the team. I told my wife when I got home that night that I had taken the team, and she was quite upset with me. I told her that the opportunity to coach the eleven- and twelve-year-old all-star team didn't occur very often so I thought I would jump on it. It turned out to be a bad choice on my part, at least for the time being.

The following day I had the first practice. I knew there were two players on the team whose fathers were assistant coaches with the teams their child played for during the regular season and that they would be happy to assist me with coaching the team. Both coaches were very knowledgeable about the game of baseball and were very friendly. I chose one of them to be the third base coach and I would leave it up to him to make the decisions for both the batters and the base runners. I offered suggestions, yet I had faith in him and felt that he had more experience than me. He graciously accepted the role. The other coach, also with previous experience, was very good at motivating the team. He kept the kids cheering during games and did a great job motivating them when they got down on themselves. I was very lucky to have these two as coaches because I never could have managed the team by myself.

One of the twelve-year-olds on the team had broken his collarbone while skateboarding two weeks before the regular season ended. He was considered to be one of the best pitchers on the all-star team and everyone hoped that he would be capable of pitching again since it was the collarbone of his pitching arm that he had broken.

I recruited a parent that was involved with the league to help work with our pitchers. He had pitched in professional baseball and was willing to show our pitchers how to throw a curve ball. During the regular season, our league allowed only fastballs, knuckle balls and change-ups. Curve balls were not allowed, so in order to compete at this next level of play the pitchers would need some quick pitching instruction.

Not only did our team not know how to throw curve balls, they also needed work on how to hit them. There were only a couple of weeks to practice before the first game, and the kids worked very hard. The players, with the exception of the eleven-year-old and one of the twelve-year-olds' who had played on the eleven- and twelve-year-old team the previous year, had played together as all-stars the previous three years and were very familiar with each others' play as well as being good friends off the field. At one of the first practices there was a minor altercation between two of the twelve-year-olds. There was a pushing match between the smallest player and the biggest player on the team. Luckily it ended very quickly. The issues were cleared up and practice resumed. There would be two rounds of play before the opportunity to compete for the State Championship. The first round was playing teams from the surrounding area. The second round covered an area that extended a bit further. The schedule for the first round was in place, and our team was ready to start.

All twelve players were available to play, including our player that had broken his collarbone. He was given the okay to play by his doctor, yet we were not in a rush for him to pitch, immediately. He was capable of playing any other position in the infield and had one of the best bats on the team.

The rules for tournament play were quite different from the rules we followed during the regular season. The rule stated that every player shall participate for a minimum of three consecutive defensive outs or bat at least one time. Any player who had been removed for a substitute could re-enter the game once, in the same position in the batting order provided his or her substitute has fulfilled his required defensive play or at bat.

The rules of pitching were much different. 1) A player could not pitch in more than nine innings in a game. 2) A player could not pitch on consecutive calendar days unless he only pitched one inning the previous day. 3) A player could pitch after one calendar day rest. 4) A player could pitch in the last game of round one and the first game of round two or the last game of round two and the first game of round three, provided he had one calendar day resting between each round. This rule allowed a pitcher to throw an incredible number of pitches, sometimes well beyond a reasonable amount. Even a twelve-year-old could injure his arm being allowed to throw that many pitches.

ROUND 1

Game 1: July 5. We were scheduled to play a team from the next town over, which was about six miles down the road. We played on their field, which had been randomly chosen at the meeting where all of the teams were paired up. They were the home team, meaning we got to bat first. Prior to the start of the game, the umpires checked out every piece of both teams' equipment to make sure they met specifications. Every baseball bat, baseball glove and baseball helmet was inspected with a fine-toothed comb. They found two bats that didn't meet specifications, a baseball glove that was considered over-sized and a helmet with a piece of protective padding missing. The catcher's gear checked out okay. That was only what they found from our team's equipment and I'm not sure if they found any flaws with our opponent's equipment. The players with the failed equipment on our team were very disturbed and had to borrow equipment from their teammates that they had never used before. It was a bad way to start off the tournament.

The pitcher that we had chosen to pitch was comparable to the player that had broken his collarbone. Most teams have a number one pitcher and a number two pitcher. We had two pitchers on our team considered as a number one pitcher. From here on, I will refer to them as Ace J and Ace K. Ace K, who we had chosen to start as pitcher, complained that his arm was a little sore. When a pitcher admits his arm is sore, it is probably very sore since they usually are not honest with the coach when asked. We decided instead to use our eleven-year-old to pitch. Ace J was the catcher, and we were finally ready to begin.

We took a 1-0 lead in the third inning after two evenly-matched innings. In the fourth inning we gave up five runs, an inning where we walked four batters, allowed two hits along with our fielders committing two errors. After four innings, it was now 5-1. The next inning we changed pitchers and held them from scoring any additional runs. We were also held scoreless, with the score remaining at 5-1. In the sixth inning, we got back only two runs, not enough to win the game. The final score was 5-3, the bad guys.

The loss put us into the loser's bracket. This was the first year the tournament was set up as double elimination. Previously, once you lost a game you were eliminated from the tournament, but this year we would have a chance to work our way back to play against the winner in the winner's bracket of the first round. It was a long road to take, since we would have to play as many as three times the number of games as the teams in the winner's bracket would have to play. There was still a chance that it could be done and our team was determined to succeed.

Game 2: July 8. This gave us a couple days to practice. We had made some position changes in the field and changes in the batting order. We decided to go with Ace J on the mound who hadn't pitched for three and one half to four weeks due to his injury. He did very well in practice, didn't complain of any soreness, and was ready to pitch again, or so he said.

Prior to the start of the game, there was a coin toss to determine who would be the home team. I always let the other manager call heads or tails. If they won the toss, they would always choose to be the home team. If I won the toss, I always chose to be the visiting team. I felt that if we batted first and scored runs first, we would be putting more pressure on the other teams, giving us an advantage. It also meant that we would bat in all six innings unless the game was shortened due to the slaughter rule. When the home team was winning the game in the sixth inning, they didn't need to bat and I thought it was better to score as many runs as possible and then rely on the defense to hold our opponents from scoring. Since the opposing team always preferred being the home team, I always started off as being a good friend of the manager of the opposing team when I elected to be the visiting team.

In the first inning of the game, our shortstop made an error on a ball hit by their first batter and Ace J allowed two hits, allowing one run to score. He then hit a batter with a pitch before getting out of the inning. It was a shaky start for Ace J in his return to pitching. The next five innings he settled down and struck out ten batters, allowed no more hits or runs, and walked five batters spread out over the five innings. He looked like he was getting back to his original self. Our team was on fire with their bats as they scored fifteen runs in six innings. They had a good night of "batting practice" winning the game 15-1. We had one day before we played our next game, giving us a day to practice.

Game 3: July 10. We chose to go back to our eleven-year-old to pitch. The team gave him a lot of support with their bats, scoring thirteen runs in only four innings. At that point, our pitcher had hit a batter with a pitch, struck out six batters, gave up a single in the third inning and a home run in the fourth inning. The game was called after four innings due to the slaughter rule. We won the game 13-1 and so far our team was headed in the right direction and picking up momentum.

Game 4: July 12. We went back to the twelve-year-old that had pitched well in the one inning he had pitched late in the first game of the tournament. Again, with only one day in between games our team was ready to play more baseball. It was the same type of game as the previous game with the same hot bats. The final score was 13-0, with the slaughter rule being called again at the end of four innings. Our pitcher walked three batters, struck out nine and allowed only one hit without giving up any runs. The kids were making good progress on the road back to the winner's bracket, with both strong pitching and hitting.

Game 5: July 14. We were scheduled to play the team that had beaten us in the first game of the tournament. We were looking for revenge and Ace K now had a well-rested arm and was ready to pitch again. After the first game, all of our games were played at a neutral site giving neither team an advantage. The previous three games had been played on a field the next town over, about twelve miles north of our town. Game 5 was scheduled to be played on the same field, which we now considered to be home for us.

The game was almost identical to our previous three games. We continued to score run after run. This time we beat our next-door neighbors in a way in that they will never forget. The final was 13-0, yet was not considered a slaughter rule, since six of our runs weren't scored until the sixth inning. The final stats for Ace K were four walks, twelve strikeouts and two hits with no runs. That was the biggest game for our team so far and a game that gave us a big boost.

After the game had ended and the team was bringing the baseball gear to my truck, one of the parents approached me in regards to his son's playing time. It was the first complaint I had received from a parent and one I knew that would come sooner or later. Every year since his son's nine-year-old year until now, his son had never shared playing time with any other player. He asked me why he wasn't playing six full innings.

I tried to be nice and I explained that he was sharing playing time since he was struggling with his hitting. If he improved, his playing time could possibly increase. It was a decision made not only by me, but also my two coaches. What parents don't understand is that at nine years old their child might be the best player on the team, yet as they get older they may not progress as fast as the other players. I continued to stay calm, yet not only did he continue to complain and get louder, but his high-school- aged daughter became involved in the conversation, also giving me a piece of her mind. While the manager beating continued, the boy's mother just stood in the background with the look of embarrassment on her face. Once her husband and daughter had finished airing their complaints, the family packed into their car with "the unhappy dad" or Tud, as I will refer to him from here after, driving the car. He made a grand exit from the ball field's parking lot, complete with tires squealing and smoking rubber in the night air.

Game 6: July 16. Again we played at the same field. The only difference was that the team we were going to play was actually from that town, and they were going to have the real home field advantage. We were going back to Ace J to pitch again. Once the game began, we felt the home field advantage still belonged to us since we continued to hit the ball hard, scored a lot of runs and played tough defense. The end result was 9-0 victory with another game to look forward to. Like our previous games, our pitching continued to be strong allowing only two walks, with eight strikeouts, only three hits and no runs. Most of the players seemed to be handling the pressure pretty well, with the exception of one child who would get sick to his stomach when the pressure seemed to be on him. He wasn't one of our pitchers but just a nervous kid. I also got the feeling that the son of one of my coaches also got a bit nervous under certain circumstances. His father would say I could take his son out of the game any time for he had played enough. That happened on more than one occasion so I wondered if the child himself wanted to come out of the game but did not want to tell me himself.

Game 7: July 18. We were scheduled again to play on our "home field". The kids were more comfortable there than they probably would have been at their real home town field. We had finally come back to play against the one remaining team in the winner's bracket. We decided to go with Ace K to face our next opponent. There was an hour-and-one-half rain delay before we could start the game, which seemed like three hours. Once the game finally began, it was not like the previous five games we had played. We knew sooner or later we would meet up with a much better team. The first inning ended with no runs scored by either team. We scored two runs in the top of the second inning and held our opponents from scoring in the bottom or the inning. The score after two complete innings was 2-0, the good guys. We added another run in the top of the third inning to take a 3-0 lead. Our opponents, another team from a town close by just to the south of us, managed to put two runs on the board to get back into the game. After three innings we still led, but only by one run, 3-2. The fourth inning was quiet for both sides, with no runs scored. In the top of the fifth inning, we managed to score another run making it 4-2. We held them again in the bottom of the fifth inning and scored one more run in the top of the sixth inning. Ace K shut them down in the bottom of the sixth inning to secure the win, 5-2. The game had been a lot closer than we had been used to and it was good for our team to come back down to earth and face reality. Again our pitcher did pretty well allowing six walks, with eleven strikeouts and only one hit, yet allowing two runs. The runs were allowed due to the four errors we made in the third inning, which was something this team rarely did.

Game 8: July 19. We had to play the same team again at the same field to see who would play in the championship game against the team from the other bracket. We decided to go with the pitcher who had pitched Game 4, Tud's son. The first inning was uneventful for both sides. The top half of the second inning produced no runs for us, yet in the bottom half of the inning, our opponents scored two runs. The bad guys led after two innings, 2-0. After two innings, Tud's son showed signs of tiredness so we decided to make a pitching change the next inning. In the third inning, we were again held scoreless. We decided to bring in Ace J in the bottom of the third. He successfully held them scoreless. We managed to get one run back in the top of the fourth inning and again Ace J held them again in the bottom of the fourth. The score after four complete innings was 2-1, with the bad guys still winning. The fifth inning was identical to the first and third inning with neither team scoring runs. We were now coming into the sixth inning, needing to score at least one run to tie and preferably a few additional insurance ones. Sure enough, Ace J hit a solo home run to tie the game at 2-2. We couldn't score any more runs but at least we had tied up. With Ace J still pitching in the bottom of the sixth, he managed to shut them down forcing the game into extra innings. Neither team could bring across any runs in the seventh inning, meaning there would be an eighth inning. We managed to bring across two runs in the top of the eighth, giving us a 4-2 lead. With Ace J still pitching in the bottom of the eighth, he started off with a strike out. Their next batter hit a home run to bring the game within one run at 4-3. Their next batter hit a single followed by the next batter grounding into a double play. The final score was 4-3, the good guys. We had two days of rest, yet we had two light practices to stay fine tuned before the big championship game.

The big day finally arrived, Game 9: July 22. We no longer had home field advantage but at least we were playing in an adjacent town only about twenty minutes away. The team we were going to play had to drive for about forty minutes to get to the field. The spectators from our town outnumbered our opponents 5:1. The reason I could tell was because of the number of spectators wearing their bright orange tee-shirts. I chose Ace K to be the starting pitcher for us. If we lost this game, there would be no tomorrow. This was our ninth game in eighteen days and everyone was looking forward to a happy ending. It had been a long road after having lost on July 5. We had played forty-six innings of baseball, scored seventy-five runs, allowed only twelve runs, and I had only one confrontation with a family.

The game was about to begin after we had lost the coin toss and were forced to be the visiting team. We jumped out to an easy 1-0 lead in the first inning and held our opponents scoreless in the bottom of the first. We added a second run in the second inning and again held them scoreless in the bottom of the second inning. The score was now 2-0. The third inning brought us another four runs as we batted through the line-up. The home team managed to score one run in the bottom of the third making the score 6-1., the good guys. In the top of the fourth inning all three of our batters grounded out to the infield. We brought in our eleven-year-old to pitch in the bottom of the fourth inning since our pitcher Ace K's arm was getting sore. The bad guys managed to get two runs back yet we still led the game 6-3 after four innings. Needing insurance runs, and after having our first three batters load up the bases, Tud's son was due to bat. He had struck out in six of his last seven at-bats and flied out in his other at-bat. I called time out and replaced him with the player he had substituted for. That player was three for three on the day and had knocked in three runs. The ball park was in complete silence as I made the change line-up. When Tud saw I was taking his son out of the game, he hollered to me "Why isn't my son going to bat, is he not feeling good?" I ignored his remark and walked back to the dugout, since I never converse with the spectators during a game. When I did not respond, he blurted out "I'm going to f--- you up after the game". Again, I ignored him. He screamed loud enough for hundreds of people at the ballpark to hear. I felt bad, not only for him, but more for his son who had heard him and must have been embarrassed.

A Glutton For Punishment

The player that I chose to replace Tud's son proceeded to hit the ball into the outfield for a single that knocked in two runs. By the end of our half of the inning we had scored five runs and were leading 11-3 after four and one half innings. Prior to our opponent's next at bat, I informed the President of our league, who was sitting about fifty feet away from Tud about the outburst. He claimed he didn't hear a thing, so I was glad I made him aware of the incident.

When the inning resumed, our opponents added another run to their total to make it an 11-4 game after five innings. We were cruising along in the top of the sixth inning with the bases loaded and one out, threatening to score more runs. We were only able to score one more run before the final two outs were made. The score after five and one-half innings was the good guys twelve and the bad guys four. Our opponent had no intention of giving up and rallied to score four quick runs making it a 12-8 game. It was time to remove our eleven-year-old who had done a good job in relief. We still needed three more outs before we would be the champions. There was a runner on third base and our new pitcher was a left-hander who was a pitcher during the regular season, but had not pitched at all in the all-star tournament. He was capable of throwing some good "junk," which meant he could throw a nasty curve ball, a dancing knuckle ball and a mean change up. He started off with a ball hit right back to him that he threw to first base, getting the runner out, after holding the runner on third base. The next batter he faced hit a pop up to the second baseman who caught it for out number two. We only needed one more out for the win. It was quiet in the ball park; you could have heard a pin drop. Even Tud was quiet. The next batter hit a ground ball to the second baseman who fielded it cleanly and threw to first base for the final out and the championship.

Two and one half weeks of baseball had resulted in winning eight games in a row after losing the first game. There was celebrating, picture-taking and sighs of relief let out by hundreds of spectators. There would be two days off prior to the start of round two and a chance to prepare for our trip down what would hopefully be a much shorter road. We still would have light practices on our two days before the next game. It was more of a time for the players to reminisce about the long road they had just traveled and the accomplishment they had made.

After we had gathered the baseball gear and were loading it into my truck, Tud appeared to let off more steam. He did not "f--- me up" but he did have a few choice words for me as he headed to his car. He left the parking lot with his tires spinning, yet there was no squealing of tires or smoking rubber since it was a gravel parking lot. Instead, rocks were flying and dirt was blowing everywhere. It looked like a mini tornado, or at least a dust storm.

Once the dust had settled, no pun intended, it was time to look forward to the next round of play. We were finally out of the losers-bracket and had a clean slate.

After the game, a pool party was held at the grandparent's house of one of the players. Everyone celebrated the victory and actually had time to relax for once. It wasn't that often that our team had a chance to get together without their baseball bats and gloves to have a little fun while taking a dip in a swimming pool.

The president of our league spoke with Tud about his behavior, and I received an apology from him. I hoped that he would continue to be on good terms with me for the rest of the summer, but only time would tell.

NEWS FLASH

July 24, one of our players showed up at practice with none other than, - a broken collarbone. He had done it the previous night while playing ice hockey. It looked like his summer of playing baseball had come to an end, and he would spend the remainder of the season sitting on the bench cheering. We would have to wait and see.

Dr. Alden

ROUND 2

Game1: July 25. The game was held back at our "home field" in the town just north of us where we had already played seven games. We chose Ace J to be our starting pitcher and pitch he did. It was a well-pitched game by both teams through five innings. Ace J had walked three batters, struck out seven, and allowed only one hit and no runs. Their pitcher did not walk a batter, struck out eight, gave up six scattered hits and no runs. In the sixth inning, we started off with a single followed by a strike out, then a fly ball to center field for out number two. Our next batter hit a double to put runners on second and third base with two outs. The next batter for us was none other than Tud's son. On the second pitch, he hit a shot up the middle for a single that brought in our runner from third base, giving us a 1-0 lead. Tud's son had finally come out of his batting slump and was very happy, as was I. Our next batter hit a ground ball to their shortstop that made the throw to first base for the final out. With only three more outs, we would have a chance to see what it was like to play in the winner's bracket.

Our opponent's first batter led off the bottom of the sixth inning with a single to left field followed by their next two batters striking out. They were down to their last out and were very patient with Ace J, who put their next batter on base with a walk. They now had runners on first and second base with hopes of a big rally. On the first pitch, their batter hit a ground ball to our shortstop, who made the throw to first base for the final out and a win. It had been quite the pitchers' duel, yet we came out on top, 1-0. The team we had just beaten was Tud's son's childhood home town. Tud was very happy for his son who had been struggling for so long with the bat, yet finally came through with his biggest hit of the summer. There was no way I was worried about being "f----- up" after that game.

Game 2: July 28. The next game provided us with completely new scenery. We played in a town roughly twelve miles southwest of us. They were not our next door neighbor, but very close to it. We had been very lucky for twelve games where we did not have to travel very far. We had three days off, which was unusual for us, and were well-prepared for what was expected to be a very close game. We came equipped with powerful bats and beat our next opponent by a score of 9-0. Ace K had pitched a good game, allowing only one hit, while striking out six batters and walking three. Our defense took care of the other twelve outs with no problems.

I will never forget this game for as long as I live due to an embarrassing situation I was put into. I had just completed hitting my fielders their pre-game warm ups on the field when I was called aside by the director of the tournament. He told me that I was not allowed on the field wearing shorts and that I would have to change into long pants unless I stayed in the dugout with my team. Since game one in the first round, I had worn a pair of khaki dress shorts and had never been told they weren't acceptable. Unfortunately for me, the league in this town we were playing in did not allow coaches to wear shorts. I would have understood if my shorts were ratty old cutoffs, but they weren't.

I did not have a pair of long pants of any sort with me, so Ace K's mother told me she had a pair of sweatpants in her car that I could borrow. The director had told me I only needed a pair of long pants, so I accepted her offer. The sweatpants were maroon and sized to fit a slim woman about five feet seven inches tall, not a heavy set man at six feet six inches tall. First, I thanked the good Lord they were not hot pink, then I proceeded to pull them up over my hefty legs and chunky waist. They were very tight on me and I looked like a moron, yet in the eyes of the tournament director they were acceptable. The maroon pants clashed with the orange and black uniforms our team was outfitted in, and I was the outcast of the team. With my new outfit on, I had only hoped that I wouldn't have to take a time out and walk onto the field to talk to my pitcher during the game. I could only imagine the look that would have come across Ace K's face as I walked out to the pitcher's mound, in his mother's sweatpants, to try and calm him down if he was having trouble pitching. Luckily, the way the game progressed, I never had to visit the mound in the presence of Ace K or the hundreds of spectators watching the game. The first thing I did the next day, was purchase a pair of khaki dress pants to be worn thereafter.

Game 3: July 30. Two days later, and still in the winner's bracket, we were ready for our next game. There were only four teams in the second round compared to almost twenty teams in the first round. Having won our first two games, we only needed to win one more game to bring home the championship of the second round. The team we were going to play for the championship had lost their first game and won their second game in round two. If we lost game 3, we would have to play the same team again.

Dr. Alden

The game was scheduled to be played west of our town in the central part of the state. It was a seventy-five mile ride, a bit longer than the twelve or so miles we were accustomed to. The team we were going to play lived the next town over and we assumed they would fill the ball park with spectators from their town. The spectators from our town packed up and traveled with us, as they had done for all of our previous games, and arrived ready to cheer on our team. With our fans wearing their bright orange tee shirts it was obvious that they outnumbered our opponent's fans by a 10:1 margin.

As the one o'clock game time approached a heavy mist in the air continued to fall, as it had all morning, with no signs of sunshine in the forecast. The weather we were experiencing was not an issue as long as it didn't turn to a heavy rain, or produce thunder and lightning. The word finally came to play ball. Just as the game was about to begin, I glanced around the complex at all of the fans from our town when I caught a glimpse of my wife who had driven to the game by herself. It was the first game she had attended since the start of the tournament play. I was glad she had finally come to a game, and I hoped there would be more games after today that she would continue to follow.

The game started about ten minutes late, since the field crew had to put the finishing touches on the damp field. The game went along as expected, with no score after the first five innings. Ace J was pitching for us, and had allowed only two batters to reach base, both via walks. We had three batters with hits and three batters getting on base with walks, yet they were scattered over the five innings with no real threats. In the sixth inning we went down one-two-three, bringing our opponents to bat in the bottom of the sixth inning. They needed to score only one run to win the game, so now it was up to our defense to hold them and give us another chance in the seventh inning. Their lead off batter got a single to start off the inning. Their next batter hit a little one hopper to the pitcher's mound that Ace J cleanly fielded but without enough time to get the lead runner heading to second base. Instead, he made the correct play; he threw to first base to get the batter out. With the heavy mist in the air and the ball being a bit damp from hitting the grass, his throw to first base slipped out of his hand and sailed over our first baseman's head into foul territory in right field. Before our right fielder had a chance to get to the ball, the runner who was on first base prior had enough time to get home and score the winning run. Game over. After the game had ended my wife came to me and said it was her fault that they lost because she jinxed them. She said she was going to leave, but after a few minutes of persuasion she agreed to stay for the next game.

Game 4: July 30. The next game was scheduled to start thirty minutes later. Both teams had a chance to rest in between games, yet were also anxious to start the next game. It was now two forty five, and the weather hadn't changed much, if anything the mist had become a little heavier. The winner of this game would be headed to round three, the state tournament. We went back to Ace K for the start and everyone was praying it would not be the team's last game of the season. The kids had never given up in the last twenty five days and did not plan to start today. I don't know why I did it, but when I won the coin toss one of my coaches persuaded me to choose to be the home team and I agreed. We had been the visiting team for so many games I only hoped it wouldn't jinx us. Maybe if we lost I could tell my wife it was my fault and not hers.

The game started out with our opponent's first batter striking out. Their next batter walked followed by their next batter getting on base after our infield made an error. This gave them runners on first and second with only one out. Their next two batters batters struck out, giving me a sigh of relief. In the bottom of the first inning we managed to get our first batter on base with a walk. Our next three batters put the ball in play but we couldn't bring across any runs before the inning ended. The second and third inning went by pretty quickly with each team getting runners on base but without scoring any runs. After three full innings the score was still tied at 0-0. In the top of the fourth inning Ace K struck out all three batters. In the bottom of the fourth our first batter struck out then our eleven-year-old walked, stole second base and went to third base on the wild throw from the catcher to second base that went into shallow center field. With our next batter up, their pitcher threw a passed ball, allowing our eleven-year-old to score. This was no surprise, as I used to say, this player ran like a deer. He was so fast running to home plate it was in only a matter of seconds that he had scored our first run of the day, and we led 1-0. After a strike out, a walk, then a force out at second base the inning ended. After four innings it was the good guys 1, the bad guys 0. Both teams were held scoreless in the fifth inning, leaving us one more inning to hold our opponents from scoring. Their first batter hit a one hopper to Ace K on the mound, who fielded the ball and threw to first base for out number one. Their next two batters struck out and we were the champions of round two.

It had been a long day. It started by traveling the seventy five miles and not knowing if the weather would cooperate long enough to play a baseball game, never mind two. Then there were the two intense games of exciting baseball. Everyone was exhausted; the players, their families, the spectators, and me. We all still had to travel seventy five miles back home, but before we could, we all had to make plans for round three. Phone calls were made from the ball field before we headed home to make lodging arrangements for the state tournament. Everything happened so fast it was like a dream. After the long ride home, one of the coaches and his wife had invited the team and their families over to their house to celebrate. The kids swam in their pool while their families, along with my wife and me, had a chance again to sit around and chat somewhere else other than on a baseball field. It had been a long, tiring day and that night everyone slept like a baby.

There were two days before our next game, and I thought we could have light practices each day just to stay fresh. At the get together the previous evening both of my coaches won out and persuaded me to give everyone a couple of days off to rest. It would give everyone time to get packed before we headed out to our next destination for round three.

I had previously discussed with my boss the possibility of needing time off from work should my team make it to the state tournament. My boss had agreed that I could take off whatever time I needed, since he thought it was great that I had devoted so much time to the kids. When I went to work the day after winning the second round championship, I got the final approval and I was off and running.

ROUND 3

Day 1: August 2. The two days off without any baseball went fast. It gave everyone a breather and the chance to get packed and prepared for what would be the end to a long summer of baseball. The players, along with most of their family members, met at our hometown ball field to travel as a caravan to our next destination, seventy miles away in the northeastern corner of the state. Some of the parents that could not get time off from their jobs would commute each afternoon after work for the games in the evening. My wife and son also joined in the caravan in my wife's car, yet would continue a little further north to visit two colleges in two different states that bordered our state. My son had just completed his junior year in high school and was looking at colleges that he might be interested in attending.

At 9:00 am, we left town for the hour and one half drive. It was a very long ride and nervousness had begun setting in for the players, their families, and even me. The tournament was scheduled to last four or five days and the players would be staying with host families in the town where the tournament was being held along with a few host families in adjacent towns. Some parents would stay in nearby hotels while others would commute from either work or home. The coaches and I were accommodated in hotel rooms provided by the league.

We arrived at the complex at 10:30 a.m. as planned. As the players got out of their parents' cars and gathered together there was a burst of laughter. They had noticed the large sign at the entrance to the complex that read, "Harry Ball Field." Needless to say, to a group of eleven- and twelve-year-olds this was quite humorous. Once they had settled down, their parents stayed with them while my coaches and I headed off to a short meeting that was scheduled for 11:00 a.m. with the other three teams that were participants in the state tournament, along with the league representatives. The tournament had started out with over one-hundred fifty teams in the state. The state was divided up into four areas. We had won round one and round two and were now in the final round to compete for the state championship.

When the meeting concluded, the players met their host families, most of whom had ball players the same age. Once our players headed to the residences of their host families the nervousness really set in and some of our players became homesick. The host families each had ideas of what to do with their guests when baseball was not on the agenda. Some had planned various activities such as swimming, bowling, visiting an amusement park or taking them out to eat. I had only asked that they did not tire out the kids since they would be playing their first game that evening at 5:00 p.m. I also asked that they would return with our players to the complex by 3:00 p.m. so they could take their pre-game batting practice prior to the opening ceremony at 4:00 p.m.

The three hours went by pretty fast and the kids arrived back to the complex at 3:00 p.m. Luckily, they didn't seem too worn out since game time was only two hours away, and it would be time again to play ball. We gave the kids their batting practice in the batting cage at the complex, and an hour later headed over to the field for the opening ceremony. The field was still quite soggy from a heavy rain storm two days earlier. There had been a second-round championship game played on the field the previous night, but only after a helicopter had been brought in to disperse the water from the field by using the force of the air flow created from the blades. My wife and son arrived at the complex in time for the opening ceremony after having spent the afternoon visiting one of the colleges. They were going to spend the night at the hotel with me, and then visit the second college the following day, returning for our second game that night.

Once the ceremony began the nervousness finally hit me. I had never been as nervous as a baseball manager as I was that afternoon. Even my first games as a Major League manager could not compare. I could tell the kids were starting to get a little more nervous too, except for Ace K. The previous year when he was eleven years old, he had played on the team representing our town that had won the state championship. The players on our team wanted to repeat as champions, which put them under even more pressure. Ace K had told our players before the ceremony how hard the team worked the previous year to become the champions and how nervous he was then as an eleven year old. He told them it was only natural to be nervous but to try and forget about it and have fun. I also tried to keep our team relaxed, trying not to let on to them how nervous I really was. After announcing the players and coaches from each of the four teams, a few words from the local dignitaries and the singing of the National Anthem it was finally time to play baseball. Our game was the first of two games that evening. The winner of each game would play each other the following evening at 7:30 p.m. and the loser of each game would play each other at 5:00 p.m.

Game 1: August 2. We had lost the coin toss at the morning meeting to our opponent who chose to be the home team. We were once again the visiting team, and I would have chosen this even if we had won the coin toss. We chose Ace J to pitch, keeping the same rotation we had followed since the start of round 2. We started off the game with a single, followed by our next two batters grounding out and an inning ending strikeout. Our opponents on the other hand had a good first inning with their lead-off batter getting a single followed by a walk to their next batter. Their next batter struck out, but two more walks followed.

To make matters worse, in the middle of it all there were two wild pitches, which allowed two runs to score. It seemed like nerves were the cause of the problems, so I changed pitchers. I brought in Ace K figuring I could go with Ace J again the next game since he had only pitched in one inning. Once Ace K came in, we made an error on their first batter that allowed another run to score, followed by a fly ball to right field for an out, which brought in another run after the catch. After walking the next batter, a line drive hit to our third baseman finally ended the inning. The end result was us being down 4-0 after one inning. To make matters worse, the director of the tournament came into our dugout during the first inning and told our team they could not cheer because it was distracting. There had not been any problems in the previous thirteen games since we had always understood that as long as it didn't distract the opposing pitcher cheering was allowed. The players had always stopped cheering before a pitch was thrown. Cheering had been a part of the game of baseball since they had been playing tee ball so it just didn't make sense. All of the sudden the dugout turned into a morgue.

Inning two we batted and went down with three ground balls to their infielders who made the plays to the first baseman for three quick outs. In the bottom of the inning we gave up two more walks, made another error in the field and threw another wild pitch giving up two more runs before getting out of the inning. The score was now, 6-0.

Inning three our first two batters struck out, with our third batter hitting a ground ball to their shortstop, who made the throw to their first baseman for out number three. The bottom of the third inning was horrendous with four walks, two passed balls and a wild pitch, allowing two more runs to score. In between the mess, seven batters had gotten up to bat and we had managed to get two outs. We then brought in our eleven-year-old to pitch. He promptly struck out the batter for the final out. It hadn't been a pretty game so far and we were now losing, 8-0.

Innings four through six we managed to get only two hits with six of our batters striking out and the other three batters barely making contact for easy outs. Inning four for the bad guys was unlike the previous three innings. All three of their batters hit ground balls to our second baseman who in turn threw to our first baseman for three quick outs. In the fifth inning their team only got one hit with two of their batters hitting ground balls to the pitcher who threw to our first baseman for the outs, then their next batter struck out. The final score of game one was 8-0.

The team we had just played had a pitcher that threw some "dirty" curve balls that we couldn't hit. We had seen some curve balls in the first two rounds of play, yet none that compared to those thrown by their pitcher. Our team was quite upset after losing the game, but my two coaches and I were positive and reminded them how they bounced back after having lost the first game of round one and winning game three of round two. We told the kids tomorrow was another day, and they would just have to start over again.

Once our players' parents had a chance to see them after the game, it was time for the players to head back to their host families' houses to spend the night. I asked the host families to have the players back to the complex by 3:00 p.m. the next day for batting practice prior to our game at 5:00 p.m. Again, I asked them not to allow the boys to do anything too strenuous so they wouldn't be tired out for the game.

That evening, my two coaches and I discussed the game plan for the next day. We agreed to go with Ace J again, hoping the nervousness had worn off and that he could return to his regular top form. Everything else would stay the same and we hoped the kids could pull through again.

Day 2: August 3. My wife and son headed out in the morning to visit the second college my son was interested in. They planned on returning in time for Game 2 at 5:00 p.m. I took a little time for myself and took a ride a few miles down the road and treated myself to some fried clams. The restaurant I went to was known for having the best fried clams in the state. I had heard about the restaurant before, but had never taken the seventy-seven mile ride it would have been from my house. The fried clams were excellent and it would be worth traveling back there again sometime, even from my hometown. I headed back to my hotel room, took a little breather, prepared the line up for the game, took a shower, got dressed and headed to the complex. I was about an hour early, but I was very anxious. The players arrived between 2:30 p.m. and 3:00 p.m. as I had asked. I spoke with each player to see how his day went. A couple of the boys stayed at a home that overlooked the ocean that they described as a mansion, while most of the other boys stayed at average or above-average homes that were described as very nice. As luck had it, my two aces, Ace J and Ace K stayed with a very nice family, but with only younger children than them. The other players all stayed with families that had boys around the same age who entertained them. Except for Ace J and Ace K, the other ten players had their own bedrooms, Ace J and Ace K each slept on his own cot in the host's living room. This resulted in an early morning visit from their host's two year old son. Unfortunately, they were prevented from sleep that their teammates were allowed to get.

The players on the team told me what they had eaten for lunch, and most of them were happy. The menu varied from seafood, which included lobster, clams, and fish and chips, to pizza or even bologna and cheese sandwiches. You probably can guess who had the bologna and cheese sandwiches. Yes, it was Ace J and Ace K. The kids also told me about the activities they did during the day. Most of them went swimming in the pools of their host families; the two boys who were staying in the "mansion" went swimming in the ocean, while a few of the other boys were entertained with other activities with the host's sons. Again, it was Ace J and Ace K who felt left out since they stayed inside the host's house playing video games all day. There wasn't much else to do, but they did tell me that when their host had to leave to do some errands, a cute high-school aged girl came to "babysit" for them and the host's children. That was the high point of the day for them. They both agreed that the best thing about being at the host family's house was that they allowed them to walk down to the corner store at 10:00 p.m. to buy frozen slush drinks. Most of the players seemed well-rested, except for Ace J and Ace K who were dragging.

It was time to think baseball again, and after a good round of batting practice the team seemed as if they were ready to go. The only player who was upset was our player who had broken his collar bone playing hockey just before round two of play was to begin. He had accompanied the team during every game of round two and had been on the bench but had not played during the first game of the state tournament. I had been told prior to batting practice that he was not allowed in the dugout unless he was going to participate in the game. His father, who happened to be one of my coaches, said the heck with it and was going to let him play the minimum requirement. He had to play either three outs on defense or get one at-bat during the game. His father said that he could take his one at bat, which made his son happy, his parents happy and his teammates happy. I was glad that he could now participate, since very few players get the opportunity to play in a state tournament.

Game 2: August 3. The team was ready, and Ace J was to take the mound as planned. We won the coin toss and again, but with the suggestion from one of my coaches, we chose to be the home team for a change. We had a very good batting practice and hoped the hitting would continue on through the game. Before the game started, I was talking to the opposing manager when he said he recognized me from a game we had played against each other the previous year. He was the manager of the same team when they were eleven-years-old and recalled that I was the manager of the 12B all star team they were playing against. He even made the comment that his team had lost to us by a score of 4-3. I honestly didn't recognize him, never mind the score. Later on I researched his claim and found it to be true.

In the top of the first inning after two quick outs, their number three batter followed with a solo home run. Their next batter struck out. In the bottom of the first inning our team came out swinging and scored two runs. It was a good sign, since we had been shut out the previous game. The score at the end of the first inning was the good guys 2 and the bad guys 1. Not much happened in the second inning with only two walks and two hits between the two teams. The score was still 2-1 after three innings. The fourth inning started out with a walk followed by a strikeout. The next batter hit a ball to our pitcher who threw to second base for a force out. With two outs, the floodgates opened. There was a passed ball, a stolen base and then three walks. This allowed a run to score. The bases were loaded and their number nine batter was up. With a count of three balls and two strikes, Ace J struck out the batter and escaped the inning with only one run scoring. The game was now tied 2-2. The bottom half of the fourth inning only lasted about three minutes. Our first batter up hit the ball back to their pitcher, who fielded the ball and threw to first base for the first out. The next batter was our player who had the broken collar bone. I substituted him into the game to get his at bat, fulfilling his playing time requirement. He laid down a perfect bunt that was fielded nicely by their pitcher, who turned and threw to first base where their second baseman was covering for out number two on a very close play. After the ball had been caught at first base, our base runner tripped over their second baseman's foot, which was on the first base bag, sending our runner flying head over heels. There was complete silence in the ball park as he hit the ground for fear that he had done more damage to his collar bone. Luckily, within seconds he was back up on his feet with a big smile on his face. He was not hurt, but happy he had the chance to play in the tournament, yet unhappy that he was not safe on the play. Our next batter was thrown out on an identical play as our first batter was for the third out. The score remained tied 2-2. The top of the fifth inning for our opponents went almost as fast as it did for us the previous inning. A few more pitches were thrown, yet their first three batters also hit the ball with each of them making an out. We started the bottom of the fifth inning at the top of our batting order. It was our turn to open the floodgates on their behalf. Our first batter got on base with a single, who then took second base on a passed ball. Our next batter also hit a single. This gave us runners on first and third base. With our next batter up, their pitcher threw another passed ball, which allowed our runner on third base to score, and move our other runner from first base to second base, giving us a 3-2 lead. Our next batter hit a double that scored the runner from second base giving us a two run lead. A line drive to their second baseman by our next batter gave us our first out. The inning finally came to an end after a walk, followed by a strikeout and then a ball hit back to the pitcher who fielded it and threw to the first baseman for the final out. The inning ended with runners left on first base and second base, but with the good guys back in the lead, 4-2 after five innings.

We only needed three more outs to get our first win in round three of play. The sixth inning for the bad guys started out with a single followed by a walk, putting runners on first and second base. We decided to make a pitching change and brought in Tud's son. The first batter he faced hit a ball back to him on the mound that he caught and threw to our third baseman for the force out. With runners on first and second base with one out, the next batter was thrown a wild pitch that advanced their runners to second and third base, respectively. I then called a time out to speak with Tud's son, who had become a bit rattled. He calmed right down and proceeded to strike out the next two batters, giving us our first win in round three. The win gave us another chance to continue on in the tournament.

Dr. Alden

The next day's headline in the local daily newspaper lauded how well our relief-pitcher did to save the game. The writer of the article was none other than Tud's daughter who was filling in for the local newspaper's sports correspondent who was unable to attend the game. She had already been writing articles as an intern with the town's weekly newspaper every week since round one. She had the perfect opportunity that day to give her brother even more exposure in the local paper. Her brother did pitch very well in relief to save the game, and I was glad that he was recognized.

Game 3 was scheduled for the next day at 4:00 p.m. It was the only game scheduled, and we would again be playing the team that had beaten us in Game 1. They had lost their second game and the winner of Game 3 would be playing against the team that had beaten them. Whichever one of us won Game 3 would have to beat that undefeated team twice in order to become the state champions. Following Game 3, a banquet for all four teams was scheduled at a local club.

After seeing their parents after the game, our players headed back to their host families' houses for the evening. Ace J and Ace K were not in a hurry to go back to their host family's house. They begged their parents to let them stay at the hotel with Ace J's parents. They only wanted to get a good night's sleep and to eat something other than sandwiches. After a lot of persuasion the boys agreed to try one more night. The hosts again were asked to follow the same rules as the previous two days, returning the players to the complex the next day at 2:00 p.m. for batting practice. That evening, my two coaches and I discussed the game plan for the next day. It was pretty simple. It would be back to Ace K again, for what we hoped would give us another "life" to get to the championship game.

Day 3: August 4. As the players arrived at the complex for their 2:00 p.m. batting practice, I checked with each of them to see how their day had gone. Their responses were similar to the previous two days with most of them a bit homesick. One of the boys wasn't feeling well, and Ace J and Ace K had the same complaints. Again they told me the best time they had was taking their 10:00 p.m. walk to the corner store for their frozen slush drinks. They told me if we won Game 3 they would not spend another night at the host family's home and insisted they would sleep at Ace J's parents' hotel room.

My son had gotten a ride home after Game 2 with one of the parents commuting to the games each day. He had visited the two colleges he wanted to see and didn't want to stay any longer. Most seventeen-year-olds are not interested in staying around for five days to watch youth baseball unless they have a brother or sister playing. My wife wanted to stay, though.

Game 3: August 4. Batting practice went well and the team seemed ready to go. Their twelve minute infield practice session before the game was also quite impressive. As in the previous game, we won the coin toss and chose to be the home team. We managed to get three hits in the first inning yet not score any runs, and had two hits in the fourth inning scoring one run. That was the extent of our hitting and run-scoring as we were totally shut down in the other four innings by their excellent pitching. We did not allow as many runs as we did in the first game we played them, but they scored enough runs to beat us. They scored three in the second inning and one run in the fourth inning while leaving fourteen runners on base. The final score, 4-1, was not as bad as the 8-0 tromping we took against them in Game 1, yet it brought an end to our season. It was tough on the kids, but once they got a chance to look back at what they had accomplished that summer, Game 3 of round three would soon be forgotten. There were a lot of tears shed at the end of the game, but an hour later at the awards banquet many of the frowns had already been replaced with smiles. The team had finished third in the state and had accomplished much more than many people thought they would. After the four teams finished their dinner, the third- and fourth-place teams received trophies for their accomplishments. The third place team trophy stood a whopping three feet tall.

Every baseball team needs a good pitching staff to be competitive and successful. Our team had much more than good pitching. We had an excellent hitting team from the top to the bottom of the batting order. The team didn't have only home-run hitters, but players that could lay down perfect bunts, and players that could put the ball in play to generate runs. Defensively, the team gelled well together and worked very hard as a team. They communicated well and made very few errors. Also, very much responsible for the success of the team were the two knowledgeable coaches that dedicated their time to the team. Last, but not least was the very supportive group of parents who provided a tremendous amount of encouragement along with the support from their families, friends and townspeople that was needed during the sixteen games in a period of thirty-two days. There was one other ingredient that made the team successful, and that was luck. A little bit of luck is necessary for every team, no matter the sport, whether it be amateur or professional. Without it, no one ever wins a championship. Throughout the tournament we experienced some luck on numerous occasions, but not quite enough. The kids never gave up after losing their first game of round one. They came back three times after losing to move forward to face their next opponent. Even in their final game of the state tournament when losing 4-0 after three and one half innings, they never gave up. It was a summer that will not be forgotten. They were a dozen boys who were not afraid to get their pants dirty while playing some very good baseball. Whether diving to make a good play defensively or hustling to get an extra base offensively, they were a team that everyone was proud of.

Almost everyone on our team went home after the awards banquet. I was very tired from the three busy days, so my wife and I decided to spend one more night at the hotel instead of making the seventy-mile trek home that evening. We thought about staying for the championship game the next day, which was at 4:00 p.m., and for the second game, if it was necessary, that would be played at 7:30 p.m.

Day 4: August 5. My wife and I decided to head home that morning. We agreed that we would wait until the results were posted in the newspaper the next day to find out who won the state championship. We figured it would be another very long day, and we could wait.

Game 4: August 5. The team that had beaten us twice won the game at 4:00 p.m. and had forced a second game at 7:30 p.m.

Game 5: August 5. They won again and were the state champions. They had fought back from the loser's bracket and won it all, as we had done in round one and round two. The team deserved to win since they were a very strong team in pitching, fielding, and batting, along with being very well coached.

17

CHILD ABUSE?

VERY HOT

Every summer the 12-B all stars was the team that couldn't seem to find tournaments without conflicts with other tournaments. I had chosen to coach the team this one particular year and found how difficult it was. We played the first weekend of the first tournament without any problems, but when the second weekend arrived and we were scheduled to play in a second tournament, it became difficult. The kids didn't mind that they would be playing a lot of baseball that weekend, but the schedule got really crazy.

It was up to me, the coach, to try to persuade the tournament directors of each tournament to accommodate our request to change the times of a game or two so that we could participate in both tournaments, concurrently. For the most part the directors worked with me the best they could, even though they were not very happy about it, yet they told me that if it wasn't possible, we would have to forfeit a game. It didn't seem fair to the kids, but I didn't have much choice in the matter.

This particular summer was one of the hottest summers in years. It was the middle of July, and we had started the first tournament with a game on a Friday night, which we won, then we played our second game of that tournament on Saturday afternoon, which we lost. It was a double elimination tournament so we were then put in the loser's bracket. Once a team went into the loser's bracket, it increased the number of games a team would have to play in order to come back and play against the team in the winner's bracket for the championship game.

The second weekend began with a game on a Thursday evening against a team from the second tournament. We won that game, which resulted in us having Friday night off from both tournaments. The following day, Saturday, was when the confusion started. The first game on Saturday was scheduled for 9:00 a.m. against our next opponent from the first tournament. The kids won the game, 6-0 and were scheduled to play at 12:00 p.m. in our next game of the second tournament. The kids packed into their parents' cars and ate a lunch their parents had prepared and drank plenty of fluids. It was about 11:15 a.m. and the temperature had already reached the mid 90's. The caravan of vehicles left the complex and within a few minutes was headed west on the Interstate for a twenty-five mile ride to the next tournament. I had bought six one-gallon jugs of water to refill the five-gallon water cooler that had started out full Saturday morning. I asked that a parent pick up a bag of ice in between games since I knew that ice water would be a hot commodity that day.

We arrived at our destination with fifteen minutes to spare and by the time the kids unloaded their gear and made their way to the field, they had a chance to sit down for five minutes. We were offered the field for our pre-game warm-ups, but we declined. We said we were all warmed-up and ready to go even though the temperature had hit 100 degrees. The only thing we were hoping for was that it did not get any hotter.

The game started on time, and the kids proceeded to win, 11-5. After the first two games of the day, the players seemed fine yet the coaches and parents were starting to drag. The kids immediately packed up their gear, hopped into their parents air-conditioned cars and headed back east on the Interstate for the twenty-five mile ride back to tournament one. The kids had a chance for a little rest, and the opportunity to re-hydrate. Luckily, there was not too much traffic headed east, but there was an accident on the west bound lane that caused a traffic backup for at least five miles. Due to the curiosity factor, traffic going our way slowed down a bit but did not cost us much time. The game had originally been scheduled to start at 2:00 p.m., but that morning I had luck getting the tournament director to move our game to 3:00 p.m. due to our previous game at noon. Again, we arrived with about fifteen minutes to spare with the temperature now at 103 degrees. The kids again unloaded their gear and were ready to play game three of the day.

A Glutton For Punishment

Again we passed up the opportunity for the pre-game warm-ups and were anxious to play yet another game. The score of the game went back and forth but the kids ended up losing, 6-3, resulting in an end to that tournament. It was a game that could have gone either way, but our day of baseball hadn't ended yet, for it was time to pack up again and head back west on the Interstate.

The team was starting to drag a bit, but hopped back into their parents' vehicles, had a snack and some fluids, and then rested until they arrived back at tournament two. We arrived in the parking lot with about three minutes to spare, got the kids and their gear to the playing field and were told that they would have to hurry up if they wanted to take their warm-ups. Warm, they were already, and as in the previous two games we declined. The tournament rule gave each team a fifteen minute window after the scheduled start time of the game, so technically we really were not late.

Game four of the day started at 6:00 p.m., and we won 7-4. The win was not as easy as game two of the day had been, yet it wasn't as intense as game three. The kids had played four games on the hottest day of July in years, and they were commended on their outstanding performance. It was about 8:15 p.m or 8:30 p.m by the time everyone headed home, and we were due back at tournament two the next morning, Sunday, for a 10:00 a.m. game.

The next morning when everyone arrived, the parents said that the kids had fallen asleep in their vehicles before they even drove out of the parking lot the previous evening. I told them that I would have done the same myself if I wasn't driving.

It was 9:00 a.m. when they arrived and the kids looked pretty well-rested considering the previous day's schedule. They were all in their clean uniforms that had probably weighed in at about twenty pounds before they had been washed, due to a day's worth of sweat and dirt. At least today there would only be one more game if they won the 10:00 a.m. game.

The kids loosened up, stretched out and actually took their pregame warm-ups on the field. It was still pretty warm at 80 degrees, but compared to the previous day, it was comfortable. The kids easily won the game 14-0 and were scheduled to play in the championship game at 12:30 p.m. The kids, their parents, their families, and the coaches had a chance to sit down for a short while and have something light to eat. It was nice not having to rush off to another field in a different town like the day before. As game time approached, the kids were back on the field preparing to bring home some "hardware". Hardware was another term for a trophy or award of some sort. Win or lose, they would be receiving hardware.

Both teams played well, with our team taking home the championship by a score of 15-5. It was closer than the score showed, and it was a good ending to a long weekend. The kids had scored twenty-seven runs on Saturday and twenty-nine runs on Sunday. That was a lot of running on two very hot days, and it would be a weekend of baseball that no one involved will forget.

HOT

The team I was coaching was a 12-B all star team, and we were playing in a tournament hosted by a town nearby. We would be playing many local teams over the course of the tournament. We had won our first game on Sunday, July 25 and also the second game we played on Friday, July 30. On Saturday, July 31, we lost our first game to an 11-A team from our town. The loss placed us in the loser's bracket, which scheduled us to play another game that afternoon, a game that we won. The win gave us the opportunity to play the 11-A team from our town a second time. A win by the 11-A team would give them the championship, and a win by us would force another game against them for the championship.

The game was scheduled for the next day, Sunday, August 1. August 1 was one of our player's thirteenth birthdays. He was a very tall, strong and intimidating boy. Aside from intentionally beaning a twelve-year-old girl in a previous tournament, he was a very good pitcher who could throw the ball very fast, yet at times could get a bit out of control in ways other than control of the ball. It was very hard to stop him once he got going, for he always seemed to be on a mission to win. I chose the birthday boy to pitch the game scheduled to start at 9:00 a.m.

He had previously pitched one inning against our local rival the day before. He had entered the game in the fifth inning with the game tied, 2-2 and ended up being the losing pitcher in s 5-2 game, after allowing three runs in that inning. I felt that if anyone on our team could beat our local rival with good pitching, it would be him. Everyone has a bad day at some point, yet I had faith in him and chose him to pitch. I also thought it would be a nice birthday gesture.

We won as our bats exploded, scoring eight runs in the game. The final score was 8-0. Our pitcher was dominant and pitched a superb game. He walked only two batters, hit one batter with a pitch, allowed only two hits and no runs with eight strikeouts in six innings. This was the best game he had ever pitched, during regular season play or during all-stars, in his youth baseball career. He was the happiest player on the team and had taken his team within one game of the championship. The championship game against our local rivals was scheduled to start after a short break.

I spoke with my coaches in regard to who I should use to pitch in the championship game. I threw out the idea of using the birthday boy again, since he was still eligible to pitch. The rules in this particular tournament allowed a player to pitch fifteen innings over the course of the tournament. He still had eight innings left that he could pitch according to the rules. I spoke with him to see how his arm felt after having just pitched six innings. His response, like that of most players, was "it feels great." I knew that would be his response, because I have never had a pitcher respond by saying "it's a little sore," or something to that effect. A player very seldom wants to admit that he has a sore arm for fear the coach won't let him play.

We decided to go with the birthday boy and hopefully make it a birthday that he would like to remember. We were the visiting team and batted first but did not score any runs. Our rivals scored two runs in the bottom of the first inning and led, 2-0. Neither team scored in the second inning, leaving the score at 2-0. In the third inning we scored two runs to tie up the game, but our local friends scored another run in the bottom of the inning to take a 3-2 lead. Nothing changed during the fourth inning, and the score remained at 3-2. We batted in the top of the fifth inning and scored a run to tie the game at 3-3. The rivals then came up to bat getting three consecutive singles that loaded the bases with no outs. I called for a time out and went out to the pitcher's mound to talk to my thirteen-year-old. He looked like he was starting to tire, but he pleaded with me to let him continue to pitch. I gave in and let him continue. He successfully struck out the next three batters, leaving the three runners stranded. We started off the sixth inning with back-to-back home runs that gave us our first lead of the game. Our next three batters went down with outs. After five and one-half innings the score was 5-3, the good guys.

I chose to put our rubber-armed pitcher back on the mound for the start of the sixth inning. I watched him very closely and would not hesitate to make a change of pitcher if so needed. The first pitch he threw was a strike, but the next four were all balls. I felt he had run out of gas, so I didn't hesitate to make a change. He had pitched eleven innings and one additional batter that day and had allowed only three runs. That was much better than the first day he faced our rivals and allowed the same number of runs, three, in only one inning. I couldn't help but let him keep pitching as long as he did, because when you're hot, you're hot.

The pitcher I brought in to relieve him got the final three outs after walking the first batter he faced. He secured a victory, the championship and a happy ending against our local rival even though they were only an eleven-year-old team. It had been a very long and tiring weekend but one that goes down in the book as one that will never be forgotten. I only hoped that the birthday boy would be able to play baseball again and that he hadn't ruined his arm for life. Sure enough, he was back on the mound again five days later to pitch in another tournament. He ended up pitching a very good game, but took a 2-0 loss due to no run support from his teammates.

Dr. Alden

SLIGHTLY UNCOMFORTABLE

What really bothered me was when a batter hit the ball into the outfield and he just stood at home plate watching the ball drop before he took off running to first base. Nine out of ten times the batter could have had a double instead of a single. I've even had a couple of batters thrown out at first by the outfielder because they didn't run as soon as they hit the ball.

It was also very common for a batter to assume that he would be out when he hit a ground ball, line drive or pop-up to an infielder. The batter would either not run at all or only run part way down to first base and then stop. To his surprise, the fielder would sometimes kick the ball, bobble the ball or drop the ball and with the batter having given up, it gave the fielder enough time to recover, make the play and get the out, where if the batter had run as soon as he hit the ball, chances are he would have been safe. There was even the possibility that when the fielder recovered to make the throw, the throw itself could have been bad and gone passed the first baseman allowing the runner to be safe.

Since these situations were very common during a game, in practice I would tell everyone not to just stand there and watch the ball but to "run their pants off" to get to the base. The meaning of that phrase was only for them to give a little extra effort in getting to the base quickly. I always stressed that they shouldn't assume anything, since you never know what is going to happen until the play has ended.

Sure enough, one day in practice a boy on my team was running so fast down the base line to first base that his pants actually fell down to his ankles. Amazingly enough he didn't seem embarrassed, and even started laughing hysterically along with the other boys on the team. Since that day I don't use that expression any longer because in this day and age I could get in serious trouble for telling a child to run his pants off, especially if it was a girl.

WARM

Whenever a player asked to go to the bathroom during a game I always responded by saying "OK, go ahead," except once. Things were a little hectic in the dugout this one particular day during the game when I told the player to, "wait just a minute". He waited but I totally forgot about his request. I didn't intentionally mean to make him wait, but it was just the response I gave since my mind was on other issues. A few minutes later, his mother came over to me in the dugout and said her son was not feeling well and that she was going to take him home.

The next time we met as a team, the child's mother explained to me what had happened. The child couldn't hold on any longer, and he wet his pants. She had taken him from the dugout, sneaked him into the boy's room, had him change into a pair of his sister's sweat pants, then whisked him off into their car and headed home. Once they got home, the nine-year-old boy was afraid his thirteen-year-old sister would see him in her sweatpants and ask why he had them on. His mother proceeded to sneak him into their house successfully accomplishing their mission and avoiding embarrassment. Once she told me the story, I felt bad for the child, and I apologized. After explaining to her what had actually happened in the dugout, she said not to worry. After that incident, I never hesitate when I hear the word "bathroom" and I always tell the child "OK, go ahead".

Dr. Alden

COOL - (NOT)

When parents send children out in the public wearing worn-out, raggedy clothes, or clothes that are years out of style, people feel bad for the children. They think it's embarrassing for the children to be seen in public with clothes of that nature. It may not have been quite the same for the tee ball division the year they received uniform shirts that had been mistakenly ordered about three sizes too big. The players wore shirts on opening day that went well below their knees and some almost to their ankles. Luckily, the correct size was ordered and arrived by rush shipment in time for the next week's games. It was only short term embarrassment yet will always be remembered by those involved.

COLD

March is not considered as baseball weather when temperatures get down into the thirties. However, managers and coaches have to get their teams outside to practice as soon as possible. There are usually only a few available weeks prior to the start of the season, and there is not much choice. Temperatures in the forties are common at the start of practices, but as the sun goes down, it tends to get quite a bit cooler. Many days, some of the players come dressed in sweatshirts or winter coats, while other players come in short-sleeved shirts. I always tell my teams and their parents that once we start outdoor practices, the players should keep a sweatshirt in their bat bag in case it gets very cold during practice or even later on once the regular season games begin. Even with the parents being present as I make the suggestion, only about half of the players carry a shirt with them. When my son played youth baseball, I would always make sure he was dressed warmly, yet not over-dressed since it would cause him embarrassment. Ten years later, parents don't seem fazed that their children are running around in a tee shirt when it is in the thirties, but question me as to how much longer practice is going to last because they, the parents, are freezing as they sit outside on the bleachers watching practice in their winter coats, with hats, scarves and gloves on. Many of the parents choose to stay in their cars during practice with their vehicle running and the heater on.

Prior to the start of the season, after teams have had a few practices, coaches like to scrimmage each others' teams. Scrimmages held after school usually continue until dark. By the time the scrimmage ends, the temperature is well into the low thirties. It seems that we, the managers and coaches, are a bit crazy, but we do what we have to do. I admit that during many early season practices when it gets cold, my hands are freezing, along with other parts of my body. I always wear my winter coat and gloves not only at practices but for the first few games into the season. I'm always happy to be able to get in my truck and crank up the heat after those cold afternoons of practices or games.

Dr. Alden

VERY COLD

Before I became a manager in the Major League division, I remember attending one of my son's Major League practices when he was eleven years old. It was a practice that I will never forget, nor will my son. My son's coach was all about practice, practice and more practice. It was mid-March and my son had practice on a day when it was 31 degrees outside. The practice started at 5:00 p.m. and was scheduled to continue until dark. The weather forecast for the day called for temperatures in the low thirties with a chance of snow flurries accompanied by windy conditions. I had cancelled my 3:30 p.m. practice right after school since it was only 33 degrees and quite windy.

Not long after my son's practice had started, the snow began to fly. It came down quite heavily and was accompanied by the predicted strong winds. The wind caused the snow to blow around so much that the players could hardly see their hands in front of them, yet practice continued. Most of the parents headed to their vehicles, if they were not already in them, turned up the heat, and put on the windshield wipers so they could continue to watch the practice. I did the same myself.

The temperature, with the wind chill factored in, had to have been down to the low twenties-no exaggeration. Practice still continued. I understood that opening day was just a couple of weeks away, but I also thought there should be a point when practice should be called off. If there was any night that a practice should have stopped, it was that evening. Not many parents were happy, and I know many of them complained. It was my son's first year in the Major League division, so I just accepted it. I had heard that if you complained, it could affect your child's playing time.

My son hadn't complained about his manager until that day when he said to me "my coach is an idiot". My son couldn't believe they practiced under those conditions and asked me to crank up the heat in my truck and get him home as quickly as possible so he could take a hot shower. I said to my son, "Welcome to the Major League". Now I understood how the Major League division was so much different from any other division in youth baseball.

Once I became a Major League manager, I swore I would never put a team of mine though what my son went through that day, no matter what.

18

The Graduate

    I've had many players on my teams over the years. Many of those I had for more than one season. There were quite a few I had on my regular season teams for four years, although some for less. As a coach, I spent many hours with them as young children. Once they moved forward, I usually didn't see them again for three or four years. Once I saw them again, they usually startled me since they had grown so much and their looks had changed. What really shocked me was when I passed them in a car that they were driving. It was amazing how fast the years went by, and my feeling was that those children that I had coached were not supposed to grow up. It only made me feel older.

    I've run into many former players since they left the youth baseball league. They recognized me, but sometimes I would run into a former player who had changed so much that he would have to tell me who he was. I remember as I came out of the post office one day, I heard a voice saying "Hi, coach". The voice was a bit deep and as I turned to say hello, I had to look almost at my eye level as I said hello to him. The individual I was speaking to was over six feet tall and was a junior in high school. I recognized him immediately, yet I shook my head in disbelief. We had a nice conversation and to think he had played on my regular season team only four, maybe five years earlier was unbelievable.

    I came upon another boy/man while standing in line at a local coffee shop. Again, a voice called out, "Hi, coach". As I turned around, I saw a bearded man only a few inches shorter than me. I had to stop and think quickly who it was. Within a few seconds, it hit me. He was one of the three cousins on my first Major League team about nine or ten years earlier. I called him by name and asked him what he was up to these days. He responded by saying that he was driving a tractor trailer up and down the eastern seaboard. Again with him, I shook my head in disbelief.

The next former player I ran into pulled up beside me at a filling station as I was pumping gasoline into my truck. He was driving a jacked up 4x4 Chevy pickup. It was so high off the ground he had to jump down about three feet in order to get out of his truck. He walked over to the pump on the opposite side of the pump I was using and said to me "Hi, coach". I knew immediately who he was since his face hadn't changed a bit since he was twelve years old. At that time, he was the smallest player on the all star state team that I was coaching six years earlier. He was now eighteen years old, a senior in high school, and not much taller.

The meeting with one individual that shocked me most occurred one Saturday morning when I had my team at the high school baseball field taking batting practice prior to our game. This person, taller than me, came over to me and said "Hello, Coach". I looked at him almost eye-to-eye and said hello. I had never coached him, but I knew immediately who he was, and I couldn't believe how tall he had gotten. It was the tall, lanky left-hander who had pitched in the Minor League division nine years earlier who every child was afraid of for fear he would be hit by his blazing fastball. He had come down to the high school to work out and run a few laps around the track to prepare himself for his junior year of college. There were also many others that I have run into over the years, about all of whom I could tell similar stories.

Every year a group of college students either on spring break, or during the summer months, stops by the ball field to play a game of home-run derby using a tennis ball. Each year there are familiar faces that show up to play, many of whom are sporting facial hair. They must want to re-live the days at the field where they spent so many hours playing youth baseball as a child. I could tell they were having a lot of fun, and I always wondered who would show up the next year. When they'd see me come down to cut the grass on the ball fields, they would always say the same thing to me, "So you're still cutting the grass on the fields and are you still coaching baseball?" My response was always "Yes, I am".

It's very hard to watch kids grow up, but that's life. I wonder what it will be like when I see them show up at the ball fields with their children to play baseball. I hope I'll still be around to see that day. That will be the day that will really make me feel old.

P.S. I never ran into Tud's son, but I heard that he had moved out of town for a while then returned part way through high school to pitch for the high school baseball team. He was chosen as a high school all-scholastic athlete in baseball and then went on to pitch for a local division-three college baseball team. He was a perfect example of the player that had his ups and downs in youth baseball, yet in his later years did very well.

19

BUILDING THE FIELDS OF DREAMS

Our league had grown to over six hundred children playing baseball, and additional baseball fields were necessary. The league had been working with the town to find a piece of land that was centrally located and large enough to accommodate at least two new baseball fields. There was a piece of land that would be ideal to build a new complex on that originally had housed a local business. When it went out of business it was acquired by the town. The parcel of land was the perfect spot. Adjacent to that property there had been a soccer field built by the local soccer association, which was also on town property.

After conferring with the soccer association, they agreed to move the soccer field onto the property that had housed the former local business. With the existing land that the soccer field had been built on and with additional land adjacent to the field was a wooded area that could be cleared out. By doing this it would be possible to build two full-sized youth baseball fields. All of this was contingent upon the town's final decision.

After two months of meetings with the town's school committee, the school building feasibility committee, the superintendent of schools and the board of selectman, the youth baseball league had finally cut through the red tape and was one step closer to building a new complex. The complex, when completed, would house the soccer field, the two new baseball fields and in the future two more fields, one being a tee ball field and the other an instructional field, once an additional wooded area had been cleared. The name chosen for the new complex was "The Fields of

Dreams," the name being used by most every town that was building new ball fields. The name came from the hit movie starring Kevin Costner, "Field of Dreams".

The next step would be to find the forces needed to remove the foundations that had remained on the property from the previous business, and who also would excavate the property to build the three new fields. I told the Board of Directors of our league at one of the general meetings that I remembered about fifteen years earlier, the National Guard built two softball fields at the local playground in town and thought that it might be worthwhile to check out the possibility of them returning to town to work on our project. The work the National Guard had performed gave the troops the opportunity to train as they built the athletic fields. The Board of Directors agreed with my idea and made numerous phone calls to the National Guard to find out what procedure we should follow to get approved. After almost two years of meetings, and much paperwork, our league received notification that we had been chosen as the recipient of the National Guard's services.

Prior to the start of any excavation the town requested that a full archaeological survey be done to determine if there were any artifacts in the area planned for excavation. Once the league had cleared all of the final hurdles, which had taken just under two more years, it was now the end of July and time for the ground-breaking ceremony. The three new fields were expected to be playable within two to three years, with an expected time frame of ten to twelve years before the whole project would be completed.

Fundraising plans were underway to generate the funds needed to complete the project. From the small businesses to the large corporations in town, all of them were solicited for donations. The league received many generous donations and had gotten off to a good start. In December, the president of the Youth Baseball league, who worked for a direct mail company, was lucky enough to have his cousin who owned the business donate their services for the printing and mailing of a brochure to every resident of the town explaining the plans that the league had for building the new complex. The goal of $250,000 was needed to cover the expenses. The end result from the mailing was quite successful, yet additional money would still have to be raised to put irrigation on the two baseball fields along with the installation of field lighting for the two fields. Batting cages were also in the plans.

Dr. Alden

My friend Pie was very instrumental in designing the complex. He had become very involved, not only as a coach, but also as a member on the Board of Directors. He spent many hours over a ten- year period visiting baseball complexes in other towns looking at the layouts of their fields. He drew up the plans for our fields and a plan for a building on our complex that would house a concession stand, a meeting room and a large hall to display the league's vast collection of awards and trophies. His design for the fields was used, but to lower the costs, the building was down-sized to house only a concession stand with a small amount of storage space upstairs. Pie was very upset when the league eliminated what he felt would have been a prized showcase.

First on the agenda was building the fields. The league was responsible for providing the fuel needed to operate all of the equipment belonging to the National Guard to be used to complete the project. Additionally, it was also our responsibility to feed the troops their lunches, snacks and dinners each day they worked on the project. The diesel fuel needed to run the equipment was donated by local oil companies, the lunches were provided by local restaurants, snacks were provided by local grocery stores and their dinners were prepared and served by members of the Youth Baseball league and the soccer association. The dinners were served in the cafeteria of an adjacent school each evening. The league figured that $80,000 - $90,000 worth of work would be provided by the National Guard once they had completed the excavation work on the project. The National Guard was only going to perform the first phase of the project with the second phase being completed by local contractors.

The National Guard successfully completed their training project in less than three weeks, and they were very proud of the end result. There was still a tremendous amount of work that had to be done. By late summer of the following year the local contractors, some of whom volunteered their services, finished the second phase of work on the fields. They were now ready for the planting of the grass seed. In September, a local landscaping company brought in machinery used to prepare the soccer field for planting. A large group of parents from both the soccer league and baseball league, armed with garden rakes, arrived and lined up from one end of the field to the other to rake out the rocks before planting the grass seed. There had to have been at least two-hundred volunteers that showed up and completed the work in only a few hours.

A few weeks later, in October, the plan was to follow the same procedure on the two baseball fields. I had strongly recommended that we wait until spring before we planted the fields, so that we would have a chance to see if the fields settled at all leaving low spots, and also to make sure there was enough pitch on the fields to give it good drainage. I remember when we built our house a few years earlier we waited until spring to make sure we had no low spots and enough pitch to direct any water away from the house. We ended up adding more fill and adjusting the grade because of the settling that had occurred. I thought it would be wise to follow the same procedure that I had used at home on the ball fields. Unfortunately, the board didn't agree with me and voted to seed the fields immediately. I tried very hard to explain how important it was to wait so we would not have puddles or an insufficient pitch so the water would drain off the fields properly. I reminded them that once we installed the fencing around the fields there would be nothing we could do to fix any problem regarding the pitch. A different landscape company from the one that volunteered on the soccer field, along with about twenty-five people from the baseball league, arrived to rake out the rocks before planting the grass seed. The turnout was nowhere near as good as the number of people who had showed up to work on the soccer field. It took two or three days to complete the job compared to the one day it took to complete the soccer field. The grass seed finally got planted and the fields were watered using a water cannon belonging to the park department that was normally used to water the town's football field during a drought.

The two new baseball fields were identical. The fields were completely enclosed by chain link fencing with the outfield fences placed at a distance of two hundred feet from home base. An infield mix comprised of a formula containing sand, clay and silt was used in the areas around the pitchers mound having a diameter of ten feet, and home base having a diameter of eighteen feet. It was also used in the sixty foot base lines running from home base to first base and from home base to third base, both having a width of four feet. Finally, it was used in the area where the base lines ran between first base and second base, and second base and third base, along with the area extending from those base lines to where the outfield would meet. Once three or four inches of the infield mix was in place grass seed was planted on the remaining areas of the fields. The new fields would have grass infields like the small one-hundred-eighty foot field located down the street from the main complex, and another two-hundred foot field located at another complex on the other side of town. Every other field the league played on had stone dust infields. The grass infields were the first step toward building a state of the art complex.

The first games were played on the new fields approximately one and one half years after the fields had been planted. My team was the first team that played on the new field, and a player on my team hit the first home run on the new field. The fields were nice, but after the first heavy rain there were puddles on the field due to low spots, and there was insufficient pitch to allow the water to run off the fields. We were now stuck with water problems forever. If only the Board of Directors had waited as I had suggested, the problems could have been corrected. Now, whenever people complain about the poorly-built fields I tell them the story as to why we have drainage problems on both baseball fields.

An irrigation system was installed on both fields a few years later, once the league could afford it. During the summer months, irrigation was needed so the fields didn't burn. The fields were beautiful in the fall, which to me is the best time of the year to play baseball. An added bonus of fall baseball is you don't have to use much water from the irrigation system during this season.

Soon after the irrigation had been installed, field lighting was installed on one of the baseball fields, and a few years later a batting cage was in place. The second field had field lighting installed a few years later. With field lighting games never had to be cut short due to darkness, and it gave some of the teams in the league the opportunity to play night games under the lights. When the league ran its summer tournament, it allowed more teams to participate, since games could be played beyond dark.

Ten years have passed since we started playing on the new fields. Nothing more has been done to continue the remainder of the project. Everything has come to a standstill until additional funding is raised.

Archaeological digs provided artifacts that dated back 6,000 years. Digs first began prior to construction in the area where the first soccer field was built, and then additional digs were performed outside of the three fields in the surrounding wooded areas. The additional digs began just prior to the start of the excavation for the new fields and continue now ten or more years later, periodically. At present, archeologists are working in an area not far from where a river passes nearby the complex. It seems as though they must be finding a good number of artifacts or they wouldn't be returning every year. At one point I was told sixty or seventy artifacts were being unearthed each day, which to me sounded like a lot.

20

MAINTAINING THE FIELDS
- THE GOOD GUY

At the October meeting, when the election of officers for the following year was held, a friend of mine (or, he used to be) nominated me for the position of Vice-President. One of the duties included maintaining all of the baseball fields. I had already served three years on the Board of Directors, two years as Player Agent and one year as Purchasing Agent. I had also just completed my first year as a Major League manager. After some discussion on what was involved with the field maintenance duties, I accepted the nomination and was unanimously elected to the position.

The cutting of the grass on the six ball fields located at three different sites had to be completed by 3:30 p.m. weekdays, which was when the first practices of the day were scheduled to begin during the regular season. Weekday games were played immediately following the practices, which normally continued up until dark. Saturday's games were scheduled all day long on all of the fields. On Sundays practices were also scheduled all day long on all the fields. The regular season practices began in March with games beginning in mid-April. The practices and games continued through the end of June, but the all-star teams began their practices and games immediately following the regular season. The all-star teams continued through at least the first week in August, and within the past two years, starting in September and continuing through mid-November, a fall baseball program was implemented that played games on Saturdays.

With this much baseball being played, the field maintenance had to be squeezed in whenever possible. The hours I worked at my job were 4:00 a.m.-12:30 p.m., with Saturdays and Sundays off, which were ideal not only for coaching baseball, but also for providing the field maintenance. I could arrive at the fields by 1:15 p.m. after work, which gave me a couple of hours each day to get the work completed.

In November, I scheduled a field clean-up day to start cleaning up the leaves and branches, which would leave less work to be done the following spring. There was a poor turnout, but some of the work did get done. The spring field clean-up day in April was scheduled and had a much better turnout of volunteers, since everyone was beginning to think about baseball. Within three or four hours, all of the fields had been cleaned up and were ready to play on. With the grass starting to grow, the league purchased a new top-of-the-line riding mower from a well-known brand name store; it had to be returned for repairs on two separate occasions. Each time the new mower broke, down I was lucky enough to have a volunteer to assist me with cutting the grass on the ball fields using his own personal riding mower, and I used my own twenty-two inch, gasoline-powered push rotary mower. The new mower never seemed to run properly even after being repaired. When it had to be returned for a third time for repairs, I suggested to the president of the league that he request a refund, since we were having so many problems with the mower. The store agreed to refund the full purchase price since the mower had been back for repairs three times in only four months.

I suggested that the league purchase a mower made specifically for cutting grass, unlike the riding mower that in all actuality was a garden tractor that could also cut grass. Additionally, I requested that the league purchase a storage trailer to be used only for the new machine and any other field maintenance equipment that only my helper and I would have access to. I asked that it be situated at the league's main complex, or complex one, as I will refer to it hereafter. Complex one consisted of one small baseball field where some of the tee ball games were played, one baseball field a little bit larger where the farm league games were played, and one baseball field that measured two-hundred feet from home base to the outfield fence where the Major League division played most of their games. There were also the two new baseball fields in the process of being built at the Fields of Dreams complex located adjacent to complex one.

The mower that I selected could cut a forty-eight inch swath and was capable of cutting the grass on a two-hundred foot field in just under one and one half hours. The mower came with a platform mounted on an axle with two wheels that was attached to the back of the frame for the operator to stand on while steering the mower. With a little practice, the mower was very easy to operate, and it made the fields look very nice after they were cut. The league had agreed to both of my requests, and I was now the official groundskeeper.

In November, an awards ceremony was held for the teams receiving trophies for the league and playoff champions, as well as for the all star teams who were recognized for their summer's accomplishments. I received the "President's Award," which was a nice embroidered jacket for all of the volunteer work I had done on the baseball fields that year. In March of the following year, I received the "Elks Distinguished Citizenship Award," which was presented to me by the local Elks lodge. I had volunteered over eight-hundred hours the previous year with the youth baseball program at the league's meetings, my regular season team's practices and games, my all star team's practices and games, along with maintaining the baseball fields. I also volunteered over two-hundred hours with the town's Sunday School Basketball League's program attending the league's meetings and coaching my son's team that had weekly practices and games. I was also responsible for refereeing a game or two, and sometimes more, each week.

After my first year of struggling to keep all of the baseball fields maintained, I requested that the league purchase a second mower with hopes that I could find a volunteer to help me out with the mowing on a regular season basis. The league agreed to purchase a mower that was a little bigger than the first mower they had purchased. It cut a fifty-two inch swath and could cut a field even faster than the forty-eight inch mower. The league also agreed to purchase a second storage trailer to be placed at another of our complexes located in the outskirts of town, which I will refer to as complex two, hereafter. There were two fields there - one measuring one-hundred-eighty feet from home base to the outfield fence and the other one, like the field at complex one, that measured two-hundred feet to the outfield fence. I decided to keep the forty-eight inch mower at complex two and use the new fifty-two inch mower at complex one since there would be much more grass to cut, especially when the two new baseball fields were completed. I had a small utility trailer donated to the league that I used to transport the mowers for repairs and to our third site that I will refer to as complex three, hereafter, when the grass needed cutting at the one-hundred-eighty foot field just down the street from complex one. It was close enough that the mower could even be driven on the street to get to the field if the utility trailer was out of order.

I was lucky and found a volunteer to help out with the two fields at complex two. Things were going pretty well until one evening when a group of hoodlums broke into the storage trailer and set it on fire. Everything in the trailer was destroyed including our year-old forty-eight inch mower. The only salvageable item to come out of the storage trailer was one of the tires and wheels from the mower's stand on platform. Luckily, the insurance company covered most of the cost of replacing the burned mower since it was only one year old. The league replaced that forty-eight inch mower with another fifty-two inch mower since the additional cost was minimal.

There was no electricity at the complex to provide illumination at night, making the complex a perfect place for kids to hang out. With the area in complete darkness, the dugouts were their favorite place to congregate to drink beer and hard liquor. They also smashed their glass bottles on the cement floor of the dugouts and smoked cigarettes and marijuana frequently. During the winter months, it was common for them to light campfires inside the dugouts to keep warm while they partied. The following year, the father of one of the nine-year-olds on my team unbolted the benches in the dugout and stored them at his house for the winter. It successfully kept the party-goers from hanging out in the dugouts once they had been removed. It wasn't that difficult for the parent since he lived only a stone's throw from the complex. The next three years there were no signs of partying but there was damage done to the roofs of the dugouts when the hoodlums tore a fence rail off the top of the fence around the ball field and used it to ram a hole through the shingles and plywood. A volunteer repaired the roofs, yet the hoodlums continued to tear off the new shingles. I recommended that a plywood roof without any shingles would be sufficient, knowing that the complex was in such an isolated area that the vandalism would only continue. Recently, a beautiful rubber roof was donated and installed on the dugouts by an individual without telling anyone. As hard as it is to believe, after two years they are still intact. I envisioned that some day the hoodlums will set them on fire and as I am cutting the grass at complex one, three miles away, I will look into the sky and see a black cloud of smoke in the direction of the dugouts with the rubber roofs.

The mischief continued year after year with incident after incident. On one occasion, a small dumpster on wheels was rolled down an incline until it crashed into the ball field's fence. From there, the culprits flipped it over the fence and rolled it out into center field. The same day, they tipped over the portable toilet after pulling out two, two-foot stakes that were driven into the ground to keep the toilet secured. The up-righting of the portable toilet was left for the company that maintained them since the mess that had been created was disgusting. Frequently, graffiti was painted on the dugouts and storage trailer, which required them to be repainted at least a couple of times a year to cover up the vulgar art work.

All things considered, the second year went pretty well since my volunteer helped out immensely with cutting the grass. Between the two of us, the six ball fields were starting to look better, and I got myself into a routine. If only I could have found a few more volunteers, I would have been very happy. Unfortunately, volunteers were hard to come by.

The following year - my third year maintaining the fields - the two new baseball fields at the Fields of Dreams complex were ready for play. It was great to get two more well-needed fields, but it also meant that I now had two more fields to maintain. There were now eight baseball fields that needed caring for, and I was lucky that the soccer field at the new Fields of Dreams complex was not my responsibility to maintain. That field would be taken care of by the soccer league themselves, thank God.

Vandalism was just as common at the other three complexes as well, even though they were centrally located in town. In addition to tipping over portable toilets and painting graffiti like the hoodlums did at complex two, they also constantly smashed the light fixtures on the concession stands and telephone poles with either rocks or BB guns. Their favorite target for destruction, though, was the picnic tables. They loved to break them up into a pile of rubble that left the remains only good enough to salvage for firewood. It was a wonder that the hoodlums did not build a bonfire themselves to destroy the evidence.

I really enjoyed cutting the grass on the fields because I loved the outdoors, it was quiet and relaxing, and I was pleased with the end result. I just cruised around the fields enjoying every minute of it, unlike many individuals who hated the thought of having to cut their grass. The only thing about the outdoors that bothered me was the bright sunshine. It was easy enough to cure, though, by wearing a pair of protective safety sunglasses while mowing and trimming or a pair of regular sunglasses while coaching. In one week, I probably cut more grass than most people cut all year. As I ride around cutting the fields, I have plenty of time to think. One day I wondered how many blades of grass there were on one ball field. I did some research and found there were 46,080 blades of grass in one square foot, therefore on one ball field having roughly 50,000 square feet of grass I figured there were 2,304,000,000 blades of grass. Kind of silly to think of something like that, I admit, but what else can one's mind think about while cruising around the ball fields? In one season, I usually collected at least one five gallon bucket of baseballs that were left on the fields, which I used the following year for soft toss. I also collected one or two dozen golf balls each year that I found hiding in the grass. Finding that many golf balls, I assumed individuals had been practicing their golf swing on those fields. A golf club can take chunks of sod out of the ground and ruin the ball field's grass. Twice I did come upon individuals practicing their game on the ball fields, and I asked them to go elsewhere, which they did without incident. If I didn't like cutting grass, I could have quit a long time ago. Very few people know who cuts the grass on the ball fields, and only a handful that do know ever comment on how they look. I can't tell you how many times one of the ball players on my teams over the years or one of the people that see me so often on the fields have asked me if I had a real job. I would tell them, I worked my real job forty to fifty hours a week and that I volunteered on the fields after I got out of work and before I started my coaching duties. I also spent many hours beginning at 6:00 a.m. on Sunday mornings working on the fields before practices started. There was also one year at complex three when I got up early one Sunday morning to finish laying down some sod that I didn't have time to do the previous day. I arrived just in time to see the sunrise on that Easter morning. I spent two-and-one-half hours putting down the remainder of the sod so I could finish the job before the sod died. I figured that I worked on the fields over four hundred hours a year. That's far more than an individual who has had a brush with the law has to fulfill performing community service. If I ever get in trouble with the law, I will be sure to tell them I've had previous experience.

I am one that feels that trimming after mowing makes all the difference in the world in the end result. At home, I always trim around the trees and along the stone walls and fences or any other place the mower couldn't cut, to put the finishing touch on the job. I spend many hours just cutting the grass on the ball fields, and I am always looking for additional volunteers to help with the trimming. Trimming along the fences after the weekly mowing of the fields is difficult for me to squeeze into my busy schedule. You would think that with over six-hundred children playing baseball in the league, it would be easy to find a few volunteers to help out. Unfortunately, I have yet to find them. The only people I did find were those who loved to complain. They were the individuals who would ask me, "When are they going to do this, or when are they going to do that?" What those people didn't understand was "they" themselves were the people that were needed to do "that". The league could use more parents, grandparents or aunts and uncles to become more involved in the league. Every year, there are only a handful of individuals like me who don't have any children or grandchildren playing in the league, yet who put in as many hours into the program as we do.

Many individuals have suggested that I spray a vegetation killer along fences so there wouldn't be a need to trim. That might work, but it would make the fields look horrible with the burned yellow grass underneath the fence compared to the nice green grass if it were trimmed regularly. A volunteer once sprayed a vegetation killer around the first and third base area where the coaches stand to kill the unwanted grass in the area. It might have worked fine had he not over-sprayed the area and killed the good grass on the ball field itself, not realizing the dead sod would have to be dug out anyway.

At one of the board meetings, a board member suggested that the league purchase a string trimmer which was set up on a four-wheel unit which looked like a lawn mower. He thought that it would be easier than using than using a weed- whacker, which to me does a real nice job with little effort as long as the trimming is done regularly. It is a little more difficult when the grass is six or eight inches tall. As much as I felt the machine wouldn't cut close enough to the fence, I curiously asked him who would operate the machine. As I expected, there was dead silence. I told the board that you could buy all the equipment you wanted, but it wasn't any good unless there was a volunteer to operate it. I had already gone through the same ordeal when someone suggested that the league purchase a small gasoline powered rotary mower to be used on the areas outside of the playing fields. I got the same response when I asked who would operate it.

With three years under my belt, I developed a routine to follow year after year. In the fall since a field clean-up day was a failure, I spent a few weeks working on the ball fields by myself in peace and quiet. I edged the infield where it met the grass in the outfield, the first and third base baselines, around the pitcher's mound and the area around the home base. I used the grass that I had edged to fill in various bare spots in the field. It took a little time, but it worked very well, and it saved the league money. In the spring, two or three weeks prior to field clean-up day, I usually did some additional work on the fields. During spring clean-up day, aside from picking up leaves and branches, there was additional work performed on the fields. Additional stone dust or infield mix was added to build up the low spots in the respective infields, holes in the outfield were filled with loam and seeded and other areas that needed tender loving care were repaired. It was also the day when the rubbish barrels were put out around the ball fields, and the advertising signs were hung on the outfield fences. I also took the day prior to opening day off from my regular job to do any last minute chores that needed to be done on the fields.

After a few years, I started taking the two days off prior to opening day. If I got behind on the field maintenance during the season, I would take an hour or two of vacation time to work on the fields. Over the course of the season, I usually used a week-and-a-half of vacation time and forfeited a few weeks worth of overtime so the kids in town could play on the best baseball fields in the area. Being so busy on the ball fields, it wasn't unusual that I neglected my own yard until the end of June, other than an occasional mowing. During the season, the grass on the ball fields had to be cut every five or six days, but during the summer months they could go a little longer if there was a lack of rain. The two ball fields that had irrigation still had to be cut as often.

I did a lot of work other than just cutting the grass on the ball fields. I aerated the fields twice a year, I fertilized the fields every six weeks, which amounted to four or five feedings a year; I took care of any weeds, moss or grub problems as they arose during the year, always avoiding the use of any harmful chemicals preferring organic substitutes. Every few years I put down a dose of garden lime on the grass in the fall if I thought it needed it. During the year I kept the mowers running properly, which meant I sharpened the blades once a week and kept the deck hosed down so the grass would eject from the machine smoothly. I also changed the oil and greased the machines once a month. If there were any repairs that needed to be done such as replacing filters, belts or any other parts that needed replacing, I took care of it myself. Very seldom did I had to send a machine out for repairs, which could turn into a huge expense.

The volunteers I've had help me with the field maintenance over the years have all done a nice job. I had one individual who helped me for four years and one who helped me for three years. Aside from those two, all of the other helpers I've had gave me two years of assistance. I'm thankful to have volunteers last for two years knowing how much time they spend working with me on the ball fields. None of my helpers ever quit on me, but just moved along with their sons to the next level of baseball. One of my helpers happened to be one of my coaches who had a son on my team. The coach, as a child, grew up not far from complex two and played baseball there as a child. He took pride in the work he did on the fields, and unfortunately only spent two years helping me before moving up to the next level of baseball to coach his son.

I also received some good help from the mother of one of the boys who played in the league. She lived directly across the street from complex one and offered to help with mowing whenever she had some extra time. She used a twenty-two inch gasoline-powered rotary mower the league purchased to cut the grass on the outside perimeter of the fields where the larger fifty-two inch mower couldn't fit. I appreciated that she always kept me posted on the work she had done, along with keeping me informed of any problems she was having with the mower.

When I got out of work, I was always in a hurry to try and cut the grass on a field or two before practices began. I knew I would have to fill the gasoline tank and check the oil before using the mower, but I was surprised when I opened the storage trailer at complex one to take out the mower. One of my helpers was going to cut the grass on one of the fields and had started to cut the field when one of the drive belts came off the machine. He put the mower back in the storage trailer with the belt just sitting on top of the mower, yet neglected to inform me of the problem he had. With the broken-down mower just sitting there waiting to be repaired, I would not have enough time to fix the mower and then cut the field I had planned on cutting before practices began. Had I known in advance, I wouldn't have been quite as upset and I could have gotten out of work a little earlier with time to fix the mower and still be able to cut the grass.

Once I was ready to start cutting the grass on the ball fields, there was always trash that needed to be picked up first before I could start mowing.

If there were cans or bottles I had to pick them up, but if there were candy wrappers or other pieces of small trash, I would just shred it up as I mowed. It would take me a half hour just to pick up all of the trash before I started mowing, but I didn't have that kind of time to waste. Very seldom would anyone pick up the trash blowing around the fields, never mind empty barrels when they got full, which usually required two people, since quite often they were filled to the top and were very heavy. Obviously, it was a dirty and smelly job, especially as the weather got warmer. Once in a while, a volunteer would sweep out the dugouts that were littered with bottles, cans, candy wrappers, sunflowers seed shells or whatever else had not been been picked up by the teams using the dugouts. Occasionally the cement floors in the dugouts were hosed down to clean up the disgusting mess that had been left behind. I tried very hard to get my team to clean up the dugout after every practice and game, since I knew how sickening the dugouts could get. I made sure the cone-shaped paper cups that were used for the drinking water I brought for the team were always picked up and put in the rubbish barrel because everyone knew I was the only manager in the league that used that style cup.

Later on, I had another incident involving another helper. He ran into a fence post with the mower and broke off one of the plastic wheels that held up the mower's deck. Again, I was not informed of the problem, and I didn't find out until I arrived at the storage trailer at complex one to use the mower to cut the grass on one of the fields, again with only a limited amount of time. I wouldn't have noticed except I happened to look in the small plastic bucket I had attached to the handle of the mower to put rocks, baseballs or other items found on the fields as we were mowing. The wheel was just sitting there without even a note to inform me of the problem.

Another time, the same individual decided to leave the storage trailer at complex one unlocked with all of the field maintenance equipment inside, while he was cutting the grass on one of the fields at the Fields of Dreams complex. The storage trailer wasn't visible from the field he was cutting, so some kids took the two unlocked padlocks that were left hanging on the doors and threw them on the roof of the storage trailer. For some unknown reason, I decided to climb up a ladder to look on the roof when I saw both padlocks lying there. Luckily, nothing was stolen from the storage trailer or damaged since that's what would usually happen in that type of situation. I always told everyone, they have to treat everything as though they were in a prison, meaning that anything and everything should be kept locked at all times. The same individual was also good at turning on the irrigation sprinklers to water the two ball fields at the Fields of Dreams complex without telling me. I repeatedly asked him to let me control the watering since there were times that his watering interfered with my mowing schedule. When he watered the fields the night before I planned on cutting the fields, the fields were still wet the next day. With an inch of water on them, the mower's drive belts would slip and the mower couldn't move. He even decided to water the fields one Friday evening, which caused the fields to be soaked for the Saturday morning games. I was so frustrated that I asked the president of the league to tell him not to touch the controls again since I felt that only one person, preferably me, should be in charge of watering the fields to avoid any type of conflict. The same individual who left me uninformed about the drive belt that had come off the mower, decided to drive a small Bobcat loader carelessly onto one of the new fields at the Fields of Dreams complex. The field was wet, which caused the machine to leave ruts and tear up the grass in the outfield, as he erratically drove the machine loaded with infield mix to the infield area. He made numerous trips back and forth causing a tremendous amount of damage to the field, unaware of what he was doing.

There was another incident that also caused some damage to the ball fields. A group of volunteers new to the league were going to do some work on one of the stone dust infields. One of the individuals drove his pick-up truck, which was towing a trailer loaded with a small Bobcat loader, onto the grass. It had rained the day before and the ball field was still wet. The truck and trailer sank into the field leaving numerous ruts. When the machine was off-loaded from the trailer additional ruts that were much worse were created. Two additional volunteers also drove their pick-up trucks onto the ball field creating even more ruts. It may not have been as noticeable to them as it was to me when I had to cut the grass. I blamed it on the lack of experience on their part along with the lack of using common sense.

The incident that bothered me most of all, literally raised my blood pressure. I had been working on the two infields at the Fields of Dreams complex a few weeks prior to field clean-up day. I had edged all of the grass along the base lines, the arc where the infield met the outfield grass and the circles around the pitcher's mounds and home bases. I had picked up the pieces of surplus grass I had edged and had spent four hours using a device to loosen up the hard-packed infield mix on one of the fields. The infield was in perfect condition and was ready to be played on.

Field clean-up day arrived, and I was unable to be there for the first two hours since I had to work at my regular job. When I did arrive, one of my field maintenance helpers was just coming off my perfect infield driving a three-ton lawn roller. He had not only rolled the grass areas of both ball fields as planned, but he also decided to roll the infield mix on both ball fields. He not only compacted the infield mix I had worked on for four hours but he also flattened out and buried the pieces of surplus grass I had edged but not yet picked up on the other infield. He also compacted the already hardened infield mix even more, which made it like cement. I was ready to kill him, but I just got back into my truck and drove away, thinking how nice he would look if I took the roller and ran him over.

There were also two incidents involving fertilizer that was supposed to have been spread by my helpers. Both times, two different years, I had brought four bags of fertilizer over to the storage trailer at complex two for the two fields that were supposed to be fertilized. Both times, I was told by my helpers that they had fertilized both fields that I had asked them to do. All four bags were needed to do both fields, but when I went into the storage trailer, both years a week later, to drop off some marking lime, I saw that two bags of fertilizer were still there, unopened. I guess they both figured they wouldn't have to cut the grass on the fields as often if they didn't use all of the fertilizer, since they probably figured it wouldn't grow as fast. I just hoped they had used at least the two bags on the ball fields and not on their own yards. Two other years, I found one bag of fertilizer missing from my storage trailer at complex one before I had fertilized any of the fields either time, making me wonder where they disappeared to.

Once the regular season had ended at the end of June, it was amazing how many people would say to me that I must be glad that the season was over so I could finally get a break. I don't know if the grass stops growing in their yards once baseball season ends, but I know the grass in my yard at home and the grass on the ball fields doesn't stop growing. In the fall we still have to cut the ball fields every five or six days due to the cool days, cool nights, and occasional rain, which causes the grass to grow even faster. What many people don't realize is that we continue cutting the fields until the end of November. It would be nice if they didn't need cutting, but that's not how it works.

Dr. Alden

There were two separate years where two different volunteers helped cut the grass on the ball fields at complex two and both of them thought the grass stopped growing at the end of the regular season. They both neglected to tell me they had stopped cutting the fields and I didn't find out until I took a ride down by the fields to check on them. Both times the grass had grown so high our grass-cutting mowers could not cut what had turned into a hay field. A heavy-duty machine had to be brought in to cut the fields both years. Had I received a phone call to let me know the grass wasn't going to be cut, I could have maintained the two additional ball fields, as much as I really wouldn't have liked to.

Five years after the two baseball fields opened at the Fields of Dreams complex, the one-hundred-eighty foot field located at complex three was no longer available for the league's use. It was the field that was originally used in town for the youth baseball program that began more than fifty years earlier. The field had been maintained by our league, but it belonged to a local veterans club. They wanted to expand their facility and use the ball field for their own functions. Losing the ball field, brought down the number of fields our league was using to seven. Granted, it was less work for me, but it provided the league, which had grown to almost seven hundred ball players, with less field availability. In the five years since the club took back their field, the grass was lucky to be cut once a month and trimming was never done. The club only used the field a matter of two, maybe three times, in the next few years, and that was for nothing more than additional parking. Singer/song writer Joni Mitchell summed it up with her song "Big Yellow Taxi" and the lyrics "Don't it always seem to go… that you don't know what you've got till it's gone…they paved paradise and put up a parking lot". Actually it hasn't been paved yet, they just drove vehicles on the lush grass creating unsightly ruts. It was depressing to me since I worked very hard year after year to maintain a beautiful complex. Luckily, a few years later, two additional practice fields were constructed, one at complex two and one located behind a school adjacent to complex one.

I must say that the kids in this town are very lucky to be able to play on baseball fields as nice as the ones we have here. Whenever I pass through a town, I always take a glance to see what type of youth baseball fields the towns have for their children to play on. There are very few that I feel are as nice as ours. Whenever my wife and I take a winter vacation to one of the many islands in the Caribbean, I always look out the shuttle bus window on our ride from the airport to the hotel to see what type of ball fields the children there play on. Every one that I ever saw was a dirt field without a single blade of grass, not even having any weeds that would at least give it a little green color. They were definitely quite different-looking than ours. To think that we complain when we have a small patch of dirt in the outfield where the grass has become worn; it's actually very minor compared to the condition of their fields. We have been told that our fields at the Fields of Dreams complex were two of the best fields in the state.

Our league hosts two tournaments every year; a nine-year-old tournament and an eleven-year-old tournament. One year we even hosted the State Tournament. In the fall prior to the year we hosted the State Tournament, we had a severe problem with grubs. Skunks in search of the grubs tore up the grass in many areas as they dug into the ground. Luckily, after treating the ball field to eliminate the grubs, the grass returned to its original thick, plush state by spring.

The following year, once the regular season had ended in June, I started working to clean up the Fields of Dreams complex, and the league started to plan to have a new sod infield put down in preparation for the State Tournament. A local landscaper was hired to prepare the infield for the new sod. With the Board of Directors agreeing with me, I recommended that additional loam be put down prior to laying the sod, since there had been numerous low spots on the infield they were replacing. I also recommended that athletic sod and not the standard household sod be used. Between the landscaper and a few individuals from the league who helped him a few nights for a few hours, the job was completed. They did not put down any additional loam because they claimed they had used a laser transit to check the pitch, which they said was fine. I could see with my naked eye there were now spots when I looked at the area, but they were supposedly right. Additionally, they didn't use the athletic sod that they claimed they were going to use. Within two years, the low spots returned on the infield and the sod did not stand up to the heavy traffic that an infield gets. The infield ended up being worse that it was before they had replaced it.

The tournament went very well, and everyone was impressed. I had spent eighty-three hours working at the complexes' two ball fields and the surrounding area prior to and during the tournament. I took a week's vacation from my regular job to be there for the league and the four teams in the tournament. The week following the tournament, an article was placed in the local newspaper giving a rundown of the tournament. A board member had written the article and mentioned how the unofficial grounds crew certainly deserved a shout. He mentioned the names of the five individuals who had been at the one ball field the few nights after work to get the facility in shape, yet neglected to mention my name. It was probably just a case of where another individual didn't know who did what around the ball fields, but noticed only what went on in front of his own nose.

Since our fields were known to be some of the best around, occasionally we were asked by surrounding towns in the area if they could use our ball fields at the Fields of Dreams complex for a tournament game, if the ball fields were available. We always agreed they could use them if our town wasn't using them.

In November, once the season fully came to an end, all of the trash barrels at all of the complexes had to be washed out and put into storage for the winter. Additionally, all of the advertising signs at all of the complexes also had to be taken down from the outfield fences and put into storage as well. Finding volunteers to do these jobs was difficult since there were fewer people available to help compared to the number of people at the spring clean-up day.

I held the position of Vice President for seven years before I declined the nomination for an eighth term. There were too many late night Board of Directors meetings, and I preferred to get a good-night's sleep. I agreed to continue to maintain the fields, which had now been going on for twelve years, but give up the Vice Presidency. Last year the league purchased its fourth grass-cutting mower which was another fifty-two inch machine just like the first one they bought but a little more updated. I plan on continuing to do what I'm doing, as long as I can find a volunteer or two to help me, hopefully in good way.

By no means were my helpers or me the only volunteers that worked at the various complexes. There were many others that did a lot of work aside from the actual field maintenance. Many repairs and other types of work were done by volunteers like me. There is one woman in particular, though, I would like to comment on. The first year in our league she managed a Farm League team and helped out with field maintenance. The next year she was elected to the Board of Directors. She held positions such as tee ball director and Farm League director over the next three years while she continued managing various teams. The following year she was elected

A Glutton For Punishment

Treasurer of the league and has continued to hold that position for thirteen years. When elected Treasurer she also helped other individuals with their positions. Over the years she assisted the Player Agents, Purchasing Agents, Umpire-in-Chief and basically anyone else that needed her help. Additionally, she ran the league's all -star tournament for thirteen years. She was often seen around the ball fields helping out in many capacities. She would hang the advertising signs on the fences in the spring, climb ladders with her bag of tools to repair the scoreboards, emptied the trash barrels and continued to help with the field maintenance. In the fall she would return to take down the advertising signs.

There are individuals that have volunteered their services for twenty five years or more in the league, as well as the woman above, who has volunteered her services for sixteen years, so far, wherever she has been needed. As I mentioned before, no one is compensated for volunteer work. The only compensation I received was when when I found an occasional penny, nickel, dime, or quarter on the fields. Once I found a five dollar bill as I was weed-whacking, but not until I had shredded it into about ten pieces, that then needed a half of a roll of scotch tape to put back together. My best pay day occurred one Sunday morning when I arrived at 5:30 a.m. to fertilize the ball fields. I found a bill that was folded up and unable to see its denomination. I figured it was probably a one dollar bill, but when I infolded it, to my surprise, it was a one-hundred dollar bill. At the time, I thought that it was a nice pay check for my twelve years of service working on the baseball fields.

21

Maintaining The Fields- The Visitors

Maintaining the baseball fields gave me the opportunity to have encounters with many visitors other than human beings. The most frustrating of all were the pet dogs. It's not that I didn't like dogs, but I had a problem when the owners of the dogs brought them down to the fields to let them run around. The ball fields were ideal since they provided a fenced-in area that gave their pets a safe environment to get exercise. Unfortunately, it was when the dogs needed to tend to their private business that created the problems. The league posted signs on all of the ball fields stating that no pets were allowed. It was obvious that dogs had been on the fields when I came upon piles of droppings as I was cutting the grass. The droppings were a health hazard to the players and coaches of the teams using the fields as well as to the students from the school adjacent to the fields. Quite often when the weather was nice, the gym teachers brought their classes outside to participate in various outdoor sports. Occasionally, teachers would also bring their classes outside to work on an assignment while sitting on the grass.

Whenever I happened to come upon a dog and its owner on the fields, I would ask the owner if they saw the signs and if they didn't I explained to them why pets were not allowed on the fields. Most everyone claimed they were carrying a bag with them to pick up the droppings knowing that someone could step on or slip on the droppings with a chance of hurting themselves. The owners may have meant well, but when a dog urinated on the fields it was impossible to clean up the urine, creating not only a health hazard but causing the area to burn and leave yellow patches throughout the fields. I would be willing to bet that the dog's owners didn't allow their pets to do their business on their own yards.

It wasn't only the local residents that chose our baseball fields to use for exercising their dogs. There have been many individuals staying at the local campgrounds while vacationing who have brought their dogs down to the fields for a visit. When I approached them they were always very upset when I asked them to leave. They gave me the same story - that it was the only place where they could let their dogs run safely since they could close the gates and keep their pets confined. Those people didn't realize how much time I spent working on the fields, because numerous times they would return the following day to let their dogs run until they saw me and decided to leave.

There was another incident involving a dog that all but made me laugh. An individual stopped to talk to me one day as I was performing some maintenance on one of the mowers not far from one of the ball fields. He said that he knew pets were not allowed on the fields but wondered if I could make an exception. He told me he had a hyper-active dog that he didn't trust to run freely and had hoped he could use the field where he could close the gates to keep his dog confined. I almost felt like telling him since there was a leash law in town, almost every dog could be claimed to be hyper-active from being confined in its house, or from only taking occasional walks on a leash with its owner. I'm sure that not every dog owner other than himself has a place of his own to let his dog run freely. Instead of getting upset with him, I bit my tongue and gave him the same answer I gave everyone else.

There were many other visitors aside from household pets. Quite often I would come upon frogs as I was cutting the grass on the ball fields. By the time they saw me, it was usually too late and the damage had been done. Frogs had a tendency to hide in blades of grass and it wasn't until I had mowed over the grass that I saw the lifeless body. Occasionally, I unintentionally ended a snake's life as I passed over it with the mower. Snakes were also a victim when I was weed whacking since I couldn't see them in the taller grass and by the time I did see them, it was usually too late. I'll never forget the day one of my helpers was trimming the grass along the fences with me. One of the advertising signs that was supposed to be attached to the fence had partially fallen on the ground and needed to be re-attached. When I picked up the corner that needed to be reattached,

I came upon a snake that was in the middle of eating his lunch. There was a mouse in the snake's mouth, half swallowed, which startled me more than it scared me. As for my helper, who was scared to death of snakes, he dropped the weed whacker he was using and said to me "I"ll see you later". I couldn't help but laugh seeing a grown man so petrified of a snake only about a foot and one half long. The only other mice I came across were those that scattered as I walked into a storage trailer.

Almost every snake I encountered was only one to two feet long, which didn't bother me. The snake that did give me a little scare was the one that had to have measured at least six feet long. I was cutting the grass on one of the ball fields when I saw the snake hurry to get out of the way of the approaching mower. The snake must have been sunning on the field that was located close to a river. I assumed that's where he was headed when I surprised him.

Other daytime visitors I frequently came upon were turtles. They had a tendency to trap themselves inside the fenced in fields and couldn't find their way out. I was more afraid of turtles than I was of snakes, since I didn't know how to tell the difference between a harmless turtle and a snapping turtle. Even if I knew, I wouldn't want to chance picking them up, since to me my fingers are a very important part of my body. Whenever I had to remove a turtle from the ball fields I always used a shovel to pick it up and then release it far enough away from the field so it wouldn't return. There were two times I was glad I used the shovel since both times they were snapping turtles and they scared me half to death when they snapped as I slid the shovel underneath them. I probably should do a little research on turtles so the next time I won't look silly if someone happens to be watching me when I jump.

The closest I came without injuring or killing a visiting family of animals occurred one afternoon as I was cutting the grass on a ball field in the area of right field. Out of the corner of my eye I happened to see a fairly good sized hole in the ground. I was just passing over the hole, so I continued until I got by before I shut down the machine. It wasn't until then that I saw four or five baby rabbits huddled together in their burrow, probably now sitting in a pile of their own poop. I was glad that I didn't harm them, and I hoped that their mother would be back soon to protect them from any other chances of getting hurt. I didn't touch them but just left them there and hoped for the best. The next day I went back to check on them, but they were not there. I thought maybe the babies had told their mother about their close call with the mower, suggesting that she move them to a safer home. I only hoped one of the many wild animals in the area didn't have a meal for himself the previous night.

In addition to the grubs, which I commented on previously, the most annoying visitors of all were the bees, wasps, mosquitoes, gnats, and herring flies. Knowing the capabilities of each of them, I would prefer to come face to face with a snake any day. Whenever I went out on the ball fields to mow or trim, I would light up a cigar and use the smoke from it to keep those pests away from me. It worked very well with an inexpensive cigar and saved me a lot of money not having to buy expensive cigars at five or ten dollars apiece. The top rails of the fences around the ball fields had a protective yellow plastic cover to prevent injuries to the ball players. It was a perfect spot for wasps to build a nest. When a ball player bumped into it or a baseball hit the fence it could upset the wasps and sometimes sting a child. If I should bump into the fence while mowing, the smoke has a tendency to keep the wasps away from me if I disturb them.

Other visitors I had to work with directly, which freaked me out at dusk, were the bats. One day I had another fifteen or twenty minutes of mowing left to do when all of a sudden what seemed like a hundred bats came out of nowhere. Their presence made me a bit nervous as they swooped down towards me. They didn't come extremely close to me, but close enough so that I felt they were playing a game of "Let's scare that guy out of his pants". They certainly did, and I hurried as fast as I could to finish cutting the grass so I could get the heck out of there. Another visitor that appeared at dusk at one of the complexes was a coyote. The coyote nonchalantly walked along the outside area beyond the outfield fence as a game was in progress. It didn't create a problem, since it just continued to walk into a wooded area. It did raise a few eyebrows and caused some concern to the players and spectators but after that brief appearance was not seen again.

There were some visitors to the fields that I got to see that most other people did not. I occasionally stopped by the fields at three or four o'clock in the morning, on my way to work, to check out the water sprinklers to make sure they came on as scheduled. I saw skunks, raccoons, foxes, a bobcat and even deer. Usually, as I pulled into the complex they would scatter, especially if I stepped outside of my truck. What really surprised me one morning as I stopped to check on the sprinklers was not an animal but a man in the outfield stark naked with a bar of soap taking a shower beside the sprinkler head. I figured it was a homeless person, so I just shook my head, got back in my truck and headed off to work. What else could I do?

What I could never understand was when the skunks and the foxes both headed underneath the storage trailer to what I assumed was where their homes were. All I could envision was that underneath the trailer there must have been a set up comparable to that of a duplex house where people live, one side for the skunks and one side for the foxes. I never did stick my head under the trailer to find out.

There were many mornings when I came down to the ball fields at 5:30 a.m. or 6:00 a.m. to work on the fields. I found it was the ideal time for the squirrels to hunt for food. As I drove into the Fields of Dreams complex to get to my storage trailer at complex one, once I came to a certain spot in the driveway, the squirrels started jumping out of every trash barrel in the complex like a jack in the box. The sound of my truck alerted them to my presence, which made me laugh every time I arrived. I felt bad for interrupting their breakfast but I'm sure they had already eaten plenty of scraps by the time I arrived. Occasionally, a few squirrels would also be seen jumping out of the trash dumpster.

There were also other visitors, and it took me fifteen minutes before I could figure out what they were. It was about 8:00 a.m. on a weekday morning when I stopped to drop off some supplies at my storage trailer at complex one. I heard a loud tapping sound coming from the area of the Fields of Dreams complex. The sound echoed through the wooded area in between the two complexes, making it difficult to find exactly where the noise was coming from. I walked over to the general vicinity that the sound was coming from, which seemed to be from the left field light tower that was used to light up the fields for night games.

At first I thought there might have been a short circuit inside the control box that would require calling an electrician. I also heard the same sound coming from the opposite side of the field. As I looked up and down the light tower to see if there were any sparks or if something was flapping in the breeze, I happened to see a bird perched near the top of the left field light tower. I figured that it must have been a woodpecker, pecking on the metal shroud around the light fixture sounding out a loud echoing tune. The noise stopped for a minute then began again, this time from the right field light tower. I waited a few more minutes as I listened to them communicate back and forth. Within a few minutes, there were at least two dozen birds that came flying over to each of the light towers. I couldn't figure out the reason the two birds were tapping out a message unless it meant it was time for them all to meet to go out for breakfast.

Many afternoons when I came down to complex one to work on the ball fields, I seemed to interrupt a woodchuck or two that must have been eating their lunch. They would scatter into the woods, or more often underneath my storage trailer. Once as I was opening the door of my storage trailer, the loud squeaking noise it made must have startled a woodchuck underneath the trailer. I looked up in time to see it come running out from underneath, fish-tailing as it made its exit. I couldn't help but laugh at the sight. Whenever I saw them at the Fields of Dreams complex, they always seemed to be enjoying one particular type of weed. When I approached them at that complex, I saw them run into the woods and down the hill towards the river. One day after grazing on one of those ball fields they apparently forgot which gate they had entered to get onto the field. They attempted to exit by digging a dozen or so areas along the outfield fence so they could crawl underneath the fence. None of the holes were deep enough for them to make their escape, therefore they must have found their way out through a gate, or maybe even climbed over the fence.

A few years after the Fields of Dreams complex was up and running, I thought it would be fitting to plant some corn outside of the outfield fences to replicate the background in the movie "The Field of Dreams". I decided after having so many visiting woodchucks and raccoons in the area, I wouldn't have much luck trying to grow corn stalks. It would have added a nice touch to the complex if it weren't for the wildlife.

I've come across many forms of wildlife during my twelve years working on the ball fields. For the most part, I have gotten along pretty well with all of them. I will continue to work along with them without disrupting their lives, but should the day arrive where I come face to face with a black bear, that will probably be the day I will decide to call it quits.

22

MAINTAINING THE FIELDS- THE BAD GUY

The April meeting, held a week-and-a-half or two weeks before opening day has the largest turnout of any meeting held over the course of the year. All managers and coaches in the league are required to attend, since part of the meeting addresses safety and basic first aid. The meeting is usually well-attended since everyone is in baseball mode. The managers also receive their game schedules, any additional equipment they had requested and first aid kits, if they did not already have one. Each member of the Board of Directors has an opportunity to address any issues he feels are important. They offer information I feel goes in one ear and out the other of many of the individuals in attendance, since many of the managers and coaches are looking forward to the start of the regular season of baseball and are not interested in their responsibilities aside from those of their games. It is also at this meeting where I give my speech on issues regarding the ball fields and the complexes they are situated on. I always thought of myself as being the bad guy, since the feeling I got from the individuals that have heard me before was that they dreaded the thought of having to listen to me address the same issues year after year. Believe me, I got tired of addressing the same issues year after year, also.

The first topic I address has to do with safety. Complex one and the Fields of Dreams complex both have ten foot gates, which when closed, prevent motor vehicles from entering the complexes. I remind the managers and coaches the reason the gates must be closed during practices and games is to protect players, their families, and everyone else from being hit by vehicular traffic. It is very easy to close the gates and hook the latches; it takes only a matter of seconds. For some reason, many managers and coaches, to this day, do not take the time to secure this area. The other issue pertaining to the gates is that managers and coaches often neglect to open the gates once the evening's activities have concluded. Leaving the gates open during the night allows police access to check on the numerous structures in the complexes.

I have been asked numerous times why I could drive my truck beyond the gates during practices and games, since no one else was allowed to. I explained that occasionally I worked on the fields or made repairs at the complexes during practices, but I always made sure I drove very slowly keeping a close eye out for pedestrians at all times. During games, I only drove my truck through the Fields of Dreams complex when their supply of marking lime had run out to pick up more marking lime at the adjacent complex one where the surplus marking lime was stored. I always made sure I had someone help direct me safely through the complexes during a situation like that. The only time I drove beyond the gate to get to my storage trailer at complex one was when it was absolutely necessary.

My next topic also involved safety. Year after year I complained about the aggressively dug holes and ditches in the outfield grass. During practices and games, players in the outfield would stand in once spot and dig with their cleats, tearing up the grass or even pulling up pieces of sod that had been put down to repair previously dug up areas. The holes and ditches made it dangerous for those running in the area. There was a day I was cutting the grass in one of the outfields when I came upon thirty two holes dug in the shape of a footprint at the Field of Dreams complex where there had been a farm league game played on a Sunday night, the previous day. For some reason, 90% of the digging usually occurred during Saturday's or Sunday's games. The year I took over the field maintenance position, I suggested to the Board of Directors that the tee ball and farm league players not be allowed to wear cleats at any time. I felt they were not necessary at those levels of play, but the Board agreed that only the tee ball players could not wear cleats. Over the years, I found that it was the farm league players that did the most damage to the fields with their legal weapons. It was bad enough when they dug on the older fields, but when the two newest and best fields at the Fields of Dreams complex were targeted, I really became upset. There was not much more I could do than to remind all managers and coaches to enforce the no digging rule.

Dr. Alden

While cutting the grass, if I noticed any areas on the ball fields that needed to be filled in with loam, I tried to do so when I'd finished mowing. If time did not allow me to, it was the manager's or coach's responsibility to check the ball field they were going to practice on or play a game on before they started in order to make sure there were no unsafe areas where a player could get hurt. Unfortunately, most managers and coaches didn't take the time to check the fields since all they wanted to do was to get started with their practice or game. There were times I told them where the areas that needed repairs were located and all that was needed was a shovelful or two of loam to prevent a ball player from twisting or breaking an ankle. Ninety percent of the time I was told O.K., yet they didn't fix the problem. What really bothered me was when a manager told me the holes would be all right because he was only having a practice. After all these years, I never knew ball players never got hurt in practices but only in games. It made more work for me, but I was usually the one that ended up filling in the holes and ditches to prevent anyone from seriously injuring himself. Many times, if I was not the one repairing the fields with loam, individuals used sand, infield mix or even stone dust to make the repairs. In cases such as that, I would have to go back and dig out the incorrect material they had used and replace it with loam.

It was not only the digging that did the damage to the fields. Occasionally, I came by the fields and found a manager or coach had a player standing on the grass in front of the backstop hitting batting practice. Having the batter stand in front of the backstop prevented foul balls from going over the backstop, which would have to be retrieved, therefore taking away valuable time from practice. The area of grass where the player was batting got ruined from the twisting and turning of the player's cleats. Since the batter was standing behind home base, the manager or coach moved up in front of the pitchers mound on the grass to pitch, which also damaged that grass from the repetitive scuffing. Another time as I passed by one of the fields, a coach who was running a practice had the players taking turns hitting a ball off a batting tee that the coach had set up in left field. The batters were hitting the balls toward the right field area, but in doing so, their cleats also ruined the area of grass where the players were batting. I always addressed those issues at the meeting, but every year I came upon a manager or coach during a practice in the process of ruining the grass. Either the manager or coach had not attended the April meeting, had forgotten what I said, or just did as he pleased. To me it was very frustrating because I was usually the one that had to make the repairs to the damaged areas.

Tryouts were always held at complex one. This had always seemed to work out well since it could accommodate all three evaluation stations within close proximity. Two years after the Fields of Dreams complex opened, the Board of Directors decided to hold tryouts at the two fields there. One field was set up to evaluate the fielding of ground balls and fly balls, while the second field was set up to evaluate the batting. It was impossible to observe the evaluations on both fields simultaneously as at complex one, where one had the capability of watching all three areas.

Evaluations went well at the nearly new complex, but by the end of the week, after hundreds of children running around in cleats, a thousand or more baseballs being hit on the grass infield to be fielded, and a thousand or more baseballs being thrown by a pitching machine to be hit, both fields received considerable damage. There were hundreds of divots on the grass infield from the repetitive hitting of ground balls, and an area of grass behind home base had worn down to the loam from having been scuffed so many times by the balls shot out of the pitching machine but not hit by the batter. I recommended that evaluations return to complex one the next year to avoid ruining the grass infields. Since the fields at complex one all had stone dust infields, which were indestructible, the Board of Directors agreed to my suggestion.

The next topic of discussion is on how to prepare the infields for practices and games. The biggest problem occurs when the managers, coaches or parents of the players rake the baselines and the infield's infield mix.

Instead of raking in the direction of first base to home base or third base to home base, they sometimes rake side to side. On grass infields it pushes the infield mix onto the grass, which causes lips to form along the baselines. Lips also form along the area where the infield meets the outfield grass when they carelessly rake or screen-drag the infield mix. Unfortunately, it's a problem that I feel will never be resolved. Stone dust infields are much easier to prepare with the only grass that could develop a lip being the area where the infield meets the outfield grass.

Once the fields have been raked, the receptacles for first base and third base need to be cleaned out before inserting the safety pop-up bases into the receptacles. Many times people do not take the time to clean them out; instead they just jump on the base hoping they meet flush with the playing area. That method does not work, instead it leaves the bases sticking up an inch or more above the surface. Again, another safety issue that is often ignored due to the lack of common sense.

On a day when the infields are puddled with water from a rain storm, additional work has to be performed prior to the final preparation of the fields. On a stone dust infield, it is usually only a matter of using a push broom to spread out the water from the puddles so that it dissipates quite quickly. Once the puddles have been spread out, it is also common to use a screen drag to further spread around the water and smooth out the field, making the field playable in no time at all. Removing puddles and drying up an infield having infield mix is much more time consuming. When the two new fields at the Fields of Dreams complex opened, I suggested that the league purchase two tarps to cover the infields when rain was expected. After a lengthy discussion, the Board of Directors chose not to purchase the tarps.

Without having tarps, the ideal situation after a night of rain is for someone to be able to come down to the fields around noon of the following day to spread out the puddles of water on the infield so the water can dissipate during the afternoon. The league purchased a manually operated device called a Super Sopper, which looks much like a typical household lawn roller. It has a highly absorbent foam pad attached to a perforated metal drum. The pad, which can soak up three quarters of an inch of water with each pass, then has the water forced out by a squeeze roller and goes into a fourteen gallon holding tank suspended on the axle. When full, the machine is rolled off the playing field and emptied. The procedure is repeated until as much water as possible has been taken off the fields. The machine was designed to be used on grass, but can be used directly on the infield mix, even though it is not recommended by the manufacturer. Once game time approaches, two or three bags of drying agent are used on each infield to dry up any areas that are still wet. More often than not, people are not available at noon to get a jump on things, so a crew has to work diligently for an hour, or sometimes longer, on each field trying to get them dry. Not having time for the infield mix to dry out means having to use almost twice as much drying agent to make the fields playable. There were even times where individuals didn't show up until a half hour before game time, expecting to use twenty bags of drying agent after pushing the sloppy muck off the infield and onto the grass. Everyone is told not to do that since over a period of time it will ruin the grass and build up a lip on the grass. The following day I am often seen on my hands and knees trying to remove the dried up slop from the grass. A rule of thumb is that if an infield needs more than five or six bags of drying agent to make it playable, then the game should be postponed. Since the drying agent costs almost fifteen dollars a bag, it is foolish to spend an outrageous amount of money just to play a game.

If there has been a day or two of continuous rain, it can take the fields with infield mix a few days before they are dry enough to play on. Note: In September of my twentieth year, the Board of Directors finally agreed to purchase one tarp that could cover the entire infield when rain was expected. They said they would try one out to see how it worked before purchasing a second one.

Once the fields have been raked and dragged, I remind everyone when they are putting down the lime for the baselines that they should run the guide string in a straight line from the back point of home base to the center of the painted foul lines on the outfield grass that are just beyond the first and third base bags. When done properly, the baselines are even with and do not extend beyond the edge of the bags. There were individuals who thought the base lines were supposed to run beside the bag, which is technically foul territory. When they put down the lime, they actually curved the base lines around the side of the bags thinking they were doing it the right way. Whenever I see it being done the wrong way, I try to explain to them nicely how to do it correctly, but quite often, they don't seemed to care.

The line machine that is used can put down either a two-inch line or a four-inch line. I tell everyone that only a two-inch line is necessary, but almost everyone still chooses to put down a four-inch line, which to them is more visible. The additional, unnecessary lime that accumulates in the baselines causes them to turn very sloppy and slippery when it gets the least bit wet. Additionally, twice as much lime means it costs the league twice as much money. Eventually, a volunteer devised a way to set up the line machines so that only a two-inch line could be put down.

I also explain to everyone that there is no need to use marking lime for the foul lines on the outfield grass since I use a special paint after each mowing that does not ruin the grass like the marking lime does. A couple of times I saw individuals putting marking lime over the paint to brighten up the lines, claiming they didn't know they were not supposed to use marking lime. I explained to them that marking lime didn't have to be used, and I never saw them do it again.

Next, I remind everyone about returning the bases and any equipment that has been used during the day back to the field storage trailers each night. It should be routine, but it is amazing how many nights the bases and the equipment used to prepare the fields are left out overnight. Not only do some people leave everything out, they also leave the trailers wide open. That is the reason I wanted a storage trailer of my own for the maintenance equipment so there would be no chance of theft. You would think since most people put away their belongings at home for the night that they would do the same at the ball fields. When the equipment is put away at the ball fields, it would be nice if the equipment was put away neatly in the trailers and locked up, but many times even when things are put away people quite often just throw everything in a pile with no concern for the next person. I know everyone is in a hurry to leave after a practice or a game, many times leaving things for the next guy or assuming the league has a good groundskeeping crew that will follow behind them and pick up their mess. It's not usually the new managers or coaches in the league as much as it is the veteran managers and coaches who have been around for years who are the biggest offenders.

Putting away equipment is nice, but helping to maintain the equipment would also be nice. People always complain about broken hand tools but there is nothing saying they can't take a few minutes to replace a nut and bolt or a screw, or to take the time to inform me nicely about a piece of broken equipment. I don't have the time to inspect every tool daily even though people think I do. Instead of telling me about a flat tire on a wheelbarrow or line machine that needs to be fixed, they wait until it has been ridden flat for so long that the tire needs to be replaced, since it is beyond repair.

According to the directions that come with the line machine, after each use the remaining lime is supposed to be emptied out and the machine hosed down with water. I would be surprised if anyone, anywhere takes the time to clean out the machine and hose it down more than once a year. That's probably why the machines don't last that long. The same neglect is also seen with our Super Sopper, which the manufacturer suggests should also be hosed down with water after each use. With the proper care, the foam pad would probably last much longer, and the holding tank wouldn't become caked-on with the hardened sand, clay and silt mixture.

A Glutton For Punishment

My final plea at the meeting is to solicit any individual that might be available to help me maintain the ball fields. I also look for individuals to help me out with trimming the grass along the fences at the baseball complexes. There usually are no volunteers. The answer I receive from most people is that they can't help out because they work. These people must think, like the players on my team and the individuals who see me so often working on the fields do, that I don't work a regular job. I totally understand that almost everyone has to work, but trimming can be done during practices on weeknights or Sundays, at their convenience. There have been individuals over the years who have told me they would help out, asking that I give them a call when I needed the help. I tell them I could use help every day since I am usually at the fields every day doing something. To make it easy, I tell them to call me when they have some free time, yet they never call. I would be willing to bet if I called them every day, they would have an excuse each time. There are times when I approach a complex with a load of marking lime, fertilizer or infield drying agent, and I try to sneak in without people seeing me coming, so I can get their help unloading the bags before they take off running. Most people are good about it, and if I can recruit one or two people to assist me, it makes my life a lot easier. With two or three people it doesn't take long to unload. After having to unload all the bags myself in the past, I learned to try to bring in the load when there would be people in the vicinity to assist me.

The league is designed to be run by volunteers. Volunteers of any sort are very hard to come by, but what bothers me most of all is that the league has to pay the umpires' salaries. Their payroll is a big expense to the league, and it's a shame they don't volunteer their services like most other individuals do. The league's rule book even states that the volunteer umpire is as much a part of the league as the volunteer manager, coach or concession stand worker, and that there is no sound reason for paying umpires.

I thought I was going to be considered a bad guy when I came upon two high-school age individuals on a ball field taking a little batting practice when I asked them if they saw the padlocks and chains I had put on the four gates leading onto the ball field. They said they did but they jumped the fence. I told them the gates were locked because the field was closed for repairs, and I'd appreciate it if they moved to another ball field close by that was available to use. They said O.K. and left. The next day I returned to cut the grass on the ball field they had vacated, and I came upon fifteen baseballs as I was mowing. I assumed they had left without picking up the baseballs they had been using the previous day. There were nine baseballs that I kept for soft toss, three that had torn covers, and three that had been shredded by my mower when I didn't see them in time. I had no idea why they didn't pick up the baseballs when they left, but I didn't complain.

I consider myself the bad guy when I find children running freely on the complexes without parental supervision and have to ask them to stop misbehaving. Children of all ages love to swing on the ten-foot gates leading into the complexes when they aren't properly secured. I have seen six or more children stand and jump on the gate causing it to sag as they swung back and forth. The weight of even small children is not intended to be placed on a gate that size, which can easily become misaligned where it meets for proper closure, resulting in the need for constant repairs.

I have also asked children not to climb the dwarf flowering trees or break off their branches. I explain that not only could they hurt themselves, but they could kill the trees. Many times when I say something to the offending children their parent or parents are standing nearby and also ask them to stop, but not before I do. What really bothers me is when a child I believe to be two or three years old throws rocks onto the ball field during a practice or game while their parent or parents are standing next to them. I've seen a child throw handfuls of rocks as their parent just watched without saying a word. I asked the child nicely to please not throw rocks over the fence and onto the grass of the ball field, as his or her parent looked at me as if I had two heads. They must have wondered who I thought I was to say that to their child. It is times like that when the parents need a good slap more than their child does. After incidents like those, I have suggested to both the older children and their parents, when visible, that the area they were at was for watching and playing baseball and not a playground.

It is not only the younger children that misbehave, but also junior-high and high-school age children as well. Rock-throwing is their favorite pastime. I have caught them on their way home from school as they passed through the complexes throwing rocks at the score boards. Not only can they do damage to the scoreboards, but all of the rocks they throw have to be picked up off the ball field's grass before I can cut the grass. I will ask them to please stop and they do, but they are only one of many groups of kids that like to play that game. I can't catch then red-handed because they quickly disappear into the woods when they see me coming from the distance. Kids that age also play a game to see who can throw the most rocks into the rubbish barrels that are standing beside the fences outside the ball fields. They get fewer rocks in the barrels than they do on the ball field's grass, leaving me anywhere between fifty and sixty rocks to pick up before I can cut the grass.

One of the most destructive acts of violence I witnessed was caused by the high school age boy I caught smashing the metal supports for the fence rail posts with a baseball bat. I heard a popping sound from the distance and went over to check on what was happening. As I approached him, before he started to run away, I threatened to call the police if I ever saw him in the complex again. Luckily, I never had another problem with him.

The other people the league doesn't like to have on the complexes are the homeless, whom I occasionally find sleeping in the dugouts. I have never woken them up to ask them to leave, but I'm sure if I did they'd be less than happy with me. Instead, I have called the police to wake them up and ask them to leave the complex. The time I was startled the most was when I looked into a dugout as I passed by while I was cutting the grass on the ball field and saw someone laying on the dugout bench. I had been mowing for a good five minutes beside the dugout before I noticed him. I wondered if he was even alive since the sound of the mower never woke him up, as far as I knew. Once I called the police, they came and woke him up and escorted him to the police cruiser in handcuffs. I assumed that he was someone they had been looking for, yet it must not have been one of the top ten most wanted criminals, since I never received a reward. Over the years numerous homeless individuals set up tents in the woods near the complexes to live in. It is an ideal location for them since there are portable toilets nearby. There is also a river not far from two of the complexes should they care to wash up, and of course, there are the automatic sprinklers close by. Whenever a tent is observed the local police are notified.

My most embarrassing moments occurred when I unintentionally intruded upon teenagers as they were examining each other's anatomy in the dugouts or on the bleachers at the ball fields. I got the feeling I was thought of as a bad guy when I surprised them at what they must have thought was a secluded area. Once I recognized a boy in the dugout as a former player in the league. I remembered him as not being a very good ball player, and one that didn't score a lot of runs. As I interrupted him with the girl he was with, again he was prevented from scoring, this time in the dugout.

Dr. Alden

With all that I have to deal with in regards to the ball fields, I have been told by a few people I should not wear a hat with the letter "M" on it, which stands for the town where I'm involved with youth baseball. They have suggested it would be more appropriate if I instead wore a hat with the letter "S" on it, for sucker. In a sense, I get a kick out of their suggestion, but quite often that is how I feel. For now, though, I'm going to continue to wear my hat with the "M" with pride.

23

ADHD

Attention-Deficit/Hyperactivity Disorder (ADHD) is a chronic condition that affects millions of children. Some of the main symptoms of ADHD are as follows. The main visible symptoms are hyperactivity and inattentiveness. Because of this, the attention span of children with ADHD is very short and they keep switching from one activity to another. They just cannot seem to focus on one thing for too long. They get bored with whatever they are doing and if they are in a group, they can distract and disrupt others with their inattention. Children with ADHD are impulsive and don't want to wait for anything. They also tend to talk a lot, which irritates everyone around them. The instinctive reaction is to yell at them, but when a child has ADHD, this is the last thing you should resort to. It's only when you realize that they cannot help themselves that you become aware that you need to deal with them differently; they just cannot behave they way the other children do.

I'm not a rocket scientist, nor am I a medical doctor, yet I'm pretty sure I can pick out a child with this condition. After having spoken with individuals who have children with it, or individuals who have worked with children having this condition, I am certain I have had many of these children with ADHD on my teams during the past twenty years.

Very seldom, have I been informed of this condition by the parents of those children with ADHD, and I have never questioned a parent. I would never have treated their child any differently than any other child, but I would have appreciated a heads up. It would have been easier on me knowing that their child might show signs of the condition so I would be able to deal with it in a professional manner and not keep me guessing. My philosophy on the youth baseball, or any youth program, is that if a child wants to participate he should be able to regardless of any issues he may have. It would be beneficial for every coach to be informed of a child's problems yet, unfortunately, many parents prefer to keep it confidential. I've been told that many parents do not give their children their medication on week-ends or during vacations. They feel that the only time their child needs the medication is while he is attending school. To me, not taking his medication is like not bringing his baseball glove to a practice or a game. A Minor League coach once told me a story about one of his players whom he knew had ADHD. He said during a game the individual was playing center field and decided to put his uniform shirt and hat on backwards, so he could turn the opposite way to watch his little brother's tee ball game at an adjacent field, thinking his coach wouldn't notice. His coach didn't notice until a ball was hit to him in center field, missing his head by six inches. It wasn't until the child turned around that his teammates hollered, and the coach realized what he had done. The outcome could have been much worse had the child gotten hit in the head.

I noticed, along with my coaches, a difference in the children on weekends compared to the way they acted during the week. Over the years, I just learned to deal with it and tried very hard not to say anything to the parents. At times it became frustrating, yet I would always remind myself that it wasn't the child's fault. In a sense, I understood the parent's reasoning, and if I had a child with ADHD, I might have done the same as a parent.

24

Extra Innings

I have coached hundreds of children in my first twenty years and have spent months at a time with most of them. When asked how many children I have, I tell people that I have a daughter, a son, two granddaughters and thirteen kids. My daughter, son and granddaughters are my pride and joy. My thirteen kids are the baseball players on my regular season team. The years that I coach an all-star team I have an additional thirteen kids that I adopt for the summer.

Between practices and games, I spend many hours during the five to six months with my thirteen regular-season players as well as many hours during the two-and-one-half months with my thirteen all-star players. Since both of my children have moved out of my house, I spend more time with the ballplayers than I spend with my own children and grandchildren.

Along with each player I also have their parents that are part of my "family". There are many different situations that I deal with as a manager. There are the married parents, the single moms, the single dads, the separated moms and dads, the divorced moms and dads, the remarried moms or dads along with step dads or step moms and even the grandparents. The toughest situation I find a child can be in is when they are in the middle of a tug-of-war. As a manager, I have had to work along with the parent and child to try to make things work smoothly.

I'm looking forward to coaching many more innings of youth baseball. I'm sure someday the time will come when I will no longer be out on the ball fields. I'll always remember the good times I had coaching, as well as the days that were a bit frustrating. One of the toughest challenges I had as a manager was keeping the team focused and not giving up when they were losing by five or more runs. I always told the kids that five runs was nothing in youth baseball. Many times we won games by scoring a few runs each inning until we came back and took the lead. It wasn't unusual to have an inning when we scored eight or ten runs. The funniest comment I ever heard was made by a ten-year-old on the team who had heard me say so many times that five runs was nothing. As I entered the dugout to give my team a pep talk before they batted in the final inning in a game where we were getting beat pretty badly, I heard the ten-year-old telling his teammates that sixteen runs was nothing in youth baseball. I honestly didn't think he was being wise, but just remembered the times when I tried to keep everyone motivated, and he was trying to motivate the team himself.

I only hope that every child that played for me enjoyed playing baseball as much as I enjoyed coaching them. In Robert Frost's poem "The Road Not Taken" he wrote, "Two roads diverged in a wood and I took the one less traveled by, and that has made all the difference". Robert Frost (March 26, 1874 - January 29, 1963)

I remember that day I ventured down the road I had never traveled that led me to the enjoyment I've had for so many years. I'll remember all the friends I made and all the friends I hope I will continue to make. I'm certain I won't forget those that were not as friendly. It's been fun to watch the children grow up as they played baseball, and it was exciting to see them succeed once they got out into the real world. Unfortunately, some did not do as well as others, and it was depressing to hear when they did not make the right decisions. Remembering them as young ballplayers made it hard to believe it was the same child.

I had the opportunity to coach in almost every division from tee ball to the Major League. The only groups that I did not coach were the eight- and-nine-year old Farm League division, and the division of youth baseball for the mentally and physically disabled youth. The disabled youths were in the range of five years old through eighteen years old, and were able to enjoy the full benefits of youth baseball in an athletic environment structured to their abilities. I have watched games played in both of these divisions and was very impressed, especially with the program provided for the disabled athletes.

Most of all, I have to thank my wife for the support and understanding she provides during baseball season. I've reminded her many times over the years how she was the one who suggested that I apply for the Major League manager position that she felt I deserved to get. I think she's kicked herself many times for that idea, since I devoted so much time to the league since that day. I'm sure she remembered what her mother went through during the years when her father was a youth baseball coach. He was a dedicated father and coach that ate, drank and slept baseball.

Should the time come when I decide to call it the end of an era, I'm sure I'll return to take a stroll down the roads I traveled so many times leading into the baseball complexes. There will still be children playing baseball with the dream of becoming a professional athlete. The grass on the fields will be as green as it was the day I moved on, with someone else taking as much pride in his work as I did to make the fields look their best. There may be different faces, or maybe even those I recognize as former ball players now coaching, yet they will be there for the same objective.

The one thing missing would be the looks on people's faces as I drove into the parking lot with my truck, which had the grill decorated with a baseball bat, baseball glove and baseball. Also missing would be the comments I received all the time about how creative it was and how they wish they had a setup like mine. The comments not only came from my home-town folks, but were also made wherever I traveled. Who knows, maybe I'll just continue displaying it forever.

I'm sure some things will never change, like the tipping over of the portable toilets, the graffiti, the personal trash of the local townspeople being placed in the dumpsters and their discarded furniture, old lawnmowers, worn out car and truck tires left at the complexes, the broken bleachers from excessive jumping, the clogged indoor toilets with rolls of toilet paper, paper towels and even rocks, the outdoor water spigots being vandalized on the buildings, the advertising signs on the ball field fences having the plastic ties intentionally snipped off so they fall on the ground, the rock-throwing at the scoreboards trying to break the light bulbs, and the list that goes on and on. I'll even miss the dump-pickers at 6:00 a.m. on a Sunday morning reaching into the dumpsters looking for returnable bottles and cans.

I'm sure there will always be issues concerning unfaithful husbands and/or wives, and any other scuttlebutt that I didn't get involved with. That was not my lifestyle as it was for many people. I stayed out of the loop when it came to situations like those, and I was probably the last person to hear anything, since all I really paid attention to was the game of baseball. Maybe in time the meteorologists will be more accurate with their weather forecasts. I was never one that listened to their reports, since they were usually wrong more than they were right. If I planned my outdoor activities around their forecasts, I probably would have never accomplished anything. I always knew the weather as soon as I walked out the door of my house and that was good enough for me. New England weather is so unpredictable there is a saying "Just wait five minutes and it will change." How meteorologist can forecast the weather for the upcoming seven days, I'll never know. What they predict and what actually happens is never the same. Even with the new sophisticated equipment that becomes available each year I tend to doubt that anything will change. When I see the sun, I know it's sunny out; when I see rain, I know it's raining out. That's pretty accurate as far as I'm concerned. Each year there are more sunny days during the baseball season than there are rainy days. If you are one that likes to get a nice sun tan, try coaching baseball. In the meantime, I'll just continue adding gray hairs to my head that were not there at the start of my coaching career. Gray is just a color to me and really doesn't bother me. I will also continue getting my tan for free unlike people that pay to go tanning booths. I assume I will also continue being told that I'm a glutton for punishment. That statement may be true after all the years of coaching and working on the ball fields, but in all actuality, it was the day that I took my sweet time getting my wife to the hospital to give birth to our daughter when I officially became "a glutton for punishment".

Epilogue

Another five years have passed since I hoped to have had this book published about my first twenty years of volunteering with youth baseball. Three years ago, the league voted that nine-year-olds would no longer be drafted onto a Major League team. I, myself liked the idea of having a child on my team for four years, which gave that child an extra year of practicing at a higher level of play. Most nine-year-olds only got the required one time at bat and played defense for the required six consecutive outs, but there have been nine-year-olds on my teams who were six-inning ballplayers. It didn't happen that often, but almost every manager has had at least one nine-year-old at one time or another who was skilled enough to play six innings.

Two years ago, I asked Rac's nineteen-year-old son if he would be interested in helping me as a coach. He had played for my team ten years ago and was in his first year of college. He was more than happy to help out and he just completed his second year as a coach with both my regular season and all-star teams. I was glad that he was willing to give his time to teach the children the game of baseball.

Also, two years ago I resigned after sixteen years of volunteer work maintaining the ball fields. I was spending more time working on the fields than I was coaching and it got to the point where I was so tired by the time my team was going to have practice or play a game, I felt that it was someone else's turn to step up to the plate so I could enjoy managing my team without always being tired.

The first year after I resigned, a few volunteers involved with the league shared the duties of maintaining the ball fields along with another individual who was paid by the league to maintain the equipment. The following year, the league hired a landscaping company to maintain the two ball fields and the area outside of the two ball fields at the Fields of Dreams complex. The other two complexes were maintained by the same few individuals who took over after me.

My twenty-fifth year was a very enjoyable year. My regular season team made it to the playoffs and were the runners-up in the championship series. So much for the saying, "Third time never fails". The kids did very well considering 8 of the 12 players on the team were first-year players on my team. One would have thought it would have been a rebuilding season, but to everyone's surprise, the team played extremely well.

Following the playoffs, I was the manager of the eleven- and twelve-year-old all-star team which participated in the tournament which had the chance to eventually compete for the state championship. The team played well, but only participated in Round 1 of play. They were beaten twice by the team who eventually won Round 1, Round 2 and the state championship. Once my team was eliminated, they participated in four different town tournaments, winning the championship at one of them and making it to the semi-finals in another. The kids still had a fun summer playing another twenty games of baseball, one game shy of what they had played during the regular season with their respective teams.

Everything else was pretty much the same during the past five years as it had been the previous twenty years. The players, the parents, the spectators, the umpires, the volunteers, and the managers and coaches didn't change much over those past five years. Only once in a while now does something happen which I haven't already seen happen. I guess youth baseball will be youth baseball.

Also, as I was entering my twenty-fifth season, my son and two of his friends decided to get involved with youth baseball. They coached a Major League team in a town about forty miles north from where my son played his first game of youth baseball as a child. Friends and relatives of mine commented as to how nice it was for him to give his time to help children, as it was for those who gave their time to coach him while playing the game that he loves so much. I guess it's like the saying, "The apple doesn't fall far from the tree".

Acknowledgments

Special thanks to Brenda Hull and Alicia Waters-Molina who shared the duties of typing my manuscript. Additionally, very special thanks to my sister, Linda Merritt and my son, Jared Sinnott for the time they spent proofreading and editing my manuscript. Also, special thanks go to my nephew, Trevor Spaulding for the time he spent as my photographer; and to my daughter, Tara Rezendes for submitting my finished product to the publishing company. And last, but not least, extra special thanks to my wife, Sue Sinnott for supporting me as a manager/coach for all of these years.

About The Author

Basketball was my favorite sport as a child. At eight years old, I started playing at home using a basketball hoop that my uncle had mounted on my family's one car garage. I played outside year- round even during the winter, once I had shoveled the snow off the driveway. I wore a pair of gloves with the fingertips cut off to help keep my hands warm. When I turned ten years old, I was old enough to play organized basketball with the local Sunday School Basketball League, which I continued playing in until the eleventh grade. I continued to play outside year-round until that time. Additionally, I played on the high school's freshman basketball team, followed by two years on the high school's junior varsity basketball team. Once I was chosen to play on the high school's varsity basketball team, I could no longer play Sunday School Basketball, since their league did not allow individuals to participate once they made the varsity team. When I went to college, I was asked by the coach of the team if I would be interested in playing basketball for him, but I graciously declined. I would have loved to play, but I chose to continue working at my part-time job to help pay my college expenses. I did manage to find enough time to play twice a week in a local men's basketball league for three years. The following year, I chose to play on a semi-professional basketball team, but just prior to the first game of the season, I injured my knee which required surgery. That ended my short stint in the league; but the following year I returned to play in the local men's basketball league for almost another twenty years, before my body told me to call it quits. Once my son was old enough to play organized basketball in the local Sunday School Basketball League at ten years old, I took the job of coaching his teams along with refereeing games. I held the position of President of the league for a number

Dr. Alden

of years until I stopped coaching in the league one year after my son graduated from high school. From that point on, even though I never played one day of true organized baseball, I focused solely on coaching baseball. I put basketball on the back burner and heavily devoted my time to America's National Pastime ever since.

My grandfather, Everett Soule teaching me how to cut grass when I was a child